STRANGE BUT TRUE!

Written by

Andrea Mills

Penguin
Random
House

Senior editor Victoria Pyke
Editor Jenny Sich
Editorial assistant Charlie Galbraith
US editor Allison Singer
Senior designer Sheila Collins
Designer David Ball
Additional design assistance
Stefan Podhorodecki, Jemma Westing
Managing editor Linda Esposito
Managing art editor Philip Letsu
Fact checking Hazel Beynon
Picture research Nic Dean, Sarah Smithies
Illustrator Stuart Jackson Carter
Creative retouching Steve Willis
Jacket design Mark Cavanagh
Jackets coordinator Claire Gell
Jacket design development manager
Sophia M Tampakopoulos Turner
Producer (pre-production) Nikoleta Parasaki
Production controller Vivienne Yong
Publisher Andrew Macintyre
Art director Karen Self
Associate publishing director Liz Wheeler
Publishing director Jonathan Metcalf

First American Edition, 2015
Published in the United States by
DK Publishing
345 Hudson Street
New York, New York 10014

A Penguin Random House Company
15 16 17 18 19 10 9 8 7 6 5 4 3 2 1
001–258601–September/2015
Copyright © 2015 Dorling Kindersley Limited

Published in Great Britain by Dorling Kindersley Limited.

A catalog record for this book is available from
the Library of Congress.
ISBN: 978-1-4654-3911-6

DK books are available at special discounts when purchased
in bulk for sales promotions, premiums, fund-raising,
or educational use. For details, contact:
DK Publishing Special Markets, 345 Hudson Street,
New York, New York 10014 or SpecialSales@dk.com.

Printed and bound in China

A WORLD OF IDEAS
SEE ALL THERE IS TO KNOW

www.dk.com

CONTENTS

What on Earth?

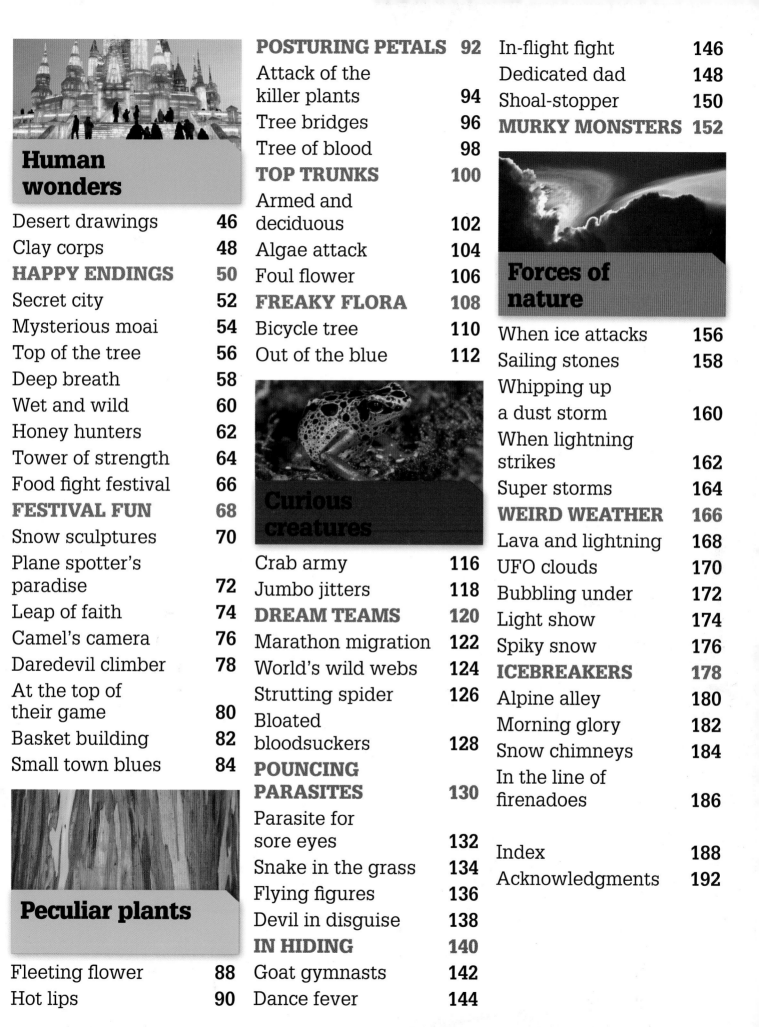

What on Earth?

Weird and wonderful places abound on our planet. Fire, air, earth, and water combine to craft some of the most unforgettable places on Earth. From glistening glaciers and an island in the clouds to multicolored mountains and forests of stone, these extraordinary environments are out of this world.

Turkey's stunning blue pools at Pamukkale (meaning "cotton castle") are produced by the region's natural hot springs. Mineral-rich waters, which are said to have healing properties, build up in rock-pool terraces.

Door to hell

Welcome to **hell on Earth**. More than 40 years ago, in the desert of north Turkmenistan, workers drilling for gas got a surprise when a **humongous hole** suddenly opened up. The resulting **crater of fire** still burns today, with locals naming the hot spot the "Door to Hell."

SUDDEN SINKHOLES

Sinkholes occur where supporting structures break down, most commonly in limestone areas. Water trickles underground, dissolving rock and creating caverns. When a cavern roof weakens, the ground opens, forming a sinkhole like this one in Guatemala.

The temperature of the burning gas is so hot, it can melt rock.

The Derweze crater is 66 ft (20 m) deep in the center and 230 ft (70 m) wide.

FAST FACTS

Sea sinkholes can occur in coastal areas. Water cuts through limestone to form caverns, into which the sinkhole collapses. If the cavern meets the sea, the level of the water in the hole rises and falls with the tide.

Sinkhole   Land   Sea

Cavern

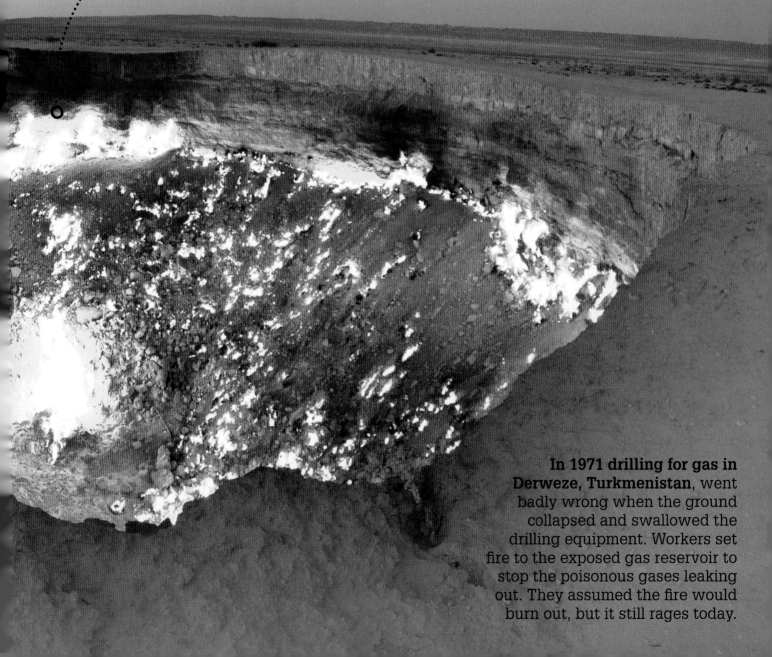

Light produced by the burning gas is visible many miles away.

In 1971 drilling for gas in Derweze, Turkmenistan, went badly wrong when the ground collapsed and swallowed the drilling equipment. Workers set fire to the exposed gas reservoir to stop the poisonous gases leaking out. They assumed the fire would burn out, but it still rages today.

Salt of the Earth

This eerie and endless **expanse of nothingness** is the **world's largest salt flat**—a dry lake bed with a perfectly flat salt crust. High on a Bolivian plateau, **Salar de Uyuni** gets covered in water when it rains. Most of this water soon evaporates, turning the surface into a **magnificent mirror**.

Stretching across 4,085 sq miles (10,582 sq km), the salt flat can be crossed on foot or by car because it is either dry or flooded by only a few centimeters of water.

SALTY STAY

Salt is so plentiful that a hotel has been built from salt in the Salar. Called Palacio de Sal ("Palace of Salt"), it dissolves in water and must be repaired every time it rains.

FAST FACTS

The Salar has a bed of salt because it has no outlet. Water collecting on the surface evaporates, leaving behind any minerals it was carrying as salts.

Ocean water Water in the open ocean is about 3.5 percent salt.

3.5% salt

Salar de Uyuni As the Salar dries up, its water becomes eight times saltier than the sea.

28% salt

Dead Sea Some salt lakes, such as the Dead Sea, are even saltier than the Salar.

33.7% salt

A thin covering of water lies over a crust of salt up to 33 ft (10 m) thick.

Highlands within the Salar become islands when the lake bed floods. The islands are never drenched, so they have no salt crust. Plants such as cacti can survive on the islands' slopes.

Beneath the salt is about half the world's supply of lithium, which is mainly used in computer and cell phone batteries.

The dry lake bed that forms Salar de Uyuni was once part of a much larger prehistoric salt lake. Occasional rainfall covers the salt briefly in water, which dissolves the surface. As the water evaporates, the salt recrystallizes in a perfectly flat plain.

A time and a place

Some places serve as reminders of the **past**. These **eerie sites** bear the scars of moments that **changed the landscape** forever.

Beach bomb
At the turn of the 20th century, the Mexican government bombed the uninhabited Marieta Islands for target practice. One bomb blasted out Hidden Beach, a postcard-picture paradise beach tucked underneath the shore.

Religious ruins
All that is left of the Mexican village of Parangaricutiro is the Church of San Juan. In 1943 the Parícutin volcano started smoking and eventually erupted, burying all the buildings except the church under rock and ash.

Unforgettable forts
In World War II, defensive forts were constructed off the UK's Kent coastline to protect the Thames estuary. The Maunsell Sea Forts are now open to the public, with boat trips to the forts offered every summer.

Lake spotting

Canada's Okanagan Valley is home to a lake **like no other**. Its dazzling dots are caused by **high levels of minerals**. For centuries **Spotted Lake** has been a **sacred site** for the First Nations (Canadian native peoples), who harnessed the **healing properties** of its mix of minerals.

WATER THERAPY

First Nations people used the lake's mud and water to treat aches, pains, and other medical problems. Legend has it that two warring tribes signed a truce so both groups could treat their injured warriors with the waters. In 2001 the Okanagan First Nations bought the site in order to protect it from development.

The lake's spots can range from green and blue to white and yellow depending on the mixture of minerals they contain.

📊 **FAST FACTS**

British Columbia, Canada

Washington, USA
Arizona, USA
Wyoming, USA
New Mexico, USA

Epsom, UK
Stassfurt, Germany
Mount Vesuvius, Italy
Hérault, France

South Africa

This map shows the main places where magnesium sulfate occurs naturally.

By the city of Osoyoos in British Columbia lies Spotted Lake. Its waters contain an unusually high concentration of minerals, especially magnesium sulfate, calcium, and sodium sulfates, along with lower levels of at least 10 other minerals. In summer the water evaporates, leaving more than 300 individual pools in an array of different colors.

Magnesium sulfate is commonly known as Epsom salts, named after the town in Surrey, UK, where the mineral also occurs naturally. It has a range of medical uses, from treating boils to relieving constipation. Many athletes bathe in Epsom salts to soothe sore muscles and speed up recovery times.

During **World War I**, the lake's **minerals** were used in Canadian ammunition factories.

Magnesium sulfate crystallizes in summer to form pathways around the lake's spots.

Mysterious wells

The **cenotes** ("sacred wells") of Mexico are **secret pools** with beautiful, clear waters. These developed naturally around the Yucatán Peninsula when **cavern roofs collapsed**. The ancient Mayan people believed cenotes were entrances to the **mysterious underworld** of the gods.

ALL THAT REMAINS

Underwater archaeologists exploring Mexico's cenotes have found human skulls and bones, suggesting that the Mayan people performed human sacrifices to honor their gods. The discoveries have scared villagers living near the cenotes today, who steer clear of these pools.

The Yucatán Peninsula is known for its porous limestone. Over time heavy rainfall caused the rock to give way in places, revealing spectacular groundwater pools underneath. The Mayans set up home nearby, making use of the pristine water supply. They thought the gods communicated at cenotes, so religious ceremonies were also performed there.

FAST FACTS

1,112 ft (339 m)

1,063 ft (324 m)

The deepest water-filled cenote in the world is also in Mexico. El Zacatón is 1,112 ft (339 m) deep—deeper than France's Eiffel Tower (1,063 ft, or 324 m) is high.

There are about 7,000 cenotes in the Yucatán Peninsula.

Tree roots dangle through the surface opening into the clear water of the cenote.

Fairy chimneys

These **magical stone structures** transform the Turkish terrain of Cappadocia into a fairy kingdom. Carved by the **forces of nature**, countless **ancient rock formations** tower over the surrounding valleys and villages.

The body of each chimney is made up of layers of limestone and volcanic ash.

Fairy chimneys are named for their seemingly magical shapes.

Fairy chimneys have explosive origins. Millions of years ago, volcanic activity resulted in layers of soft sedimentary rock, topped by a hard layer of basalt. At the mercy of wind and rain, the soft rock eroded gradually, transforming the landscape into distinctive shapes, including cones, columns, and mushrooms. Local people turned the chimneys into buildings, shaping houses, churches, and monasteries out of the rock.

FAIRYTALE HOTELS

Some of the larger fairy chimneys have been hollowed out and sculpted into unique boutique hotels. With cave-like rooms offering views of the colossal chimneys, visitors can enjoy the most authentic experience of Cappadocia.

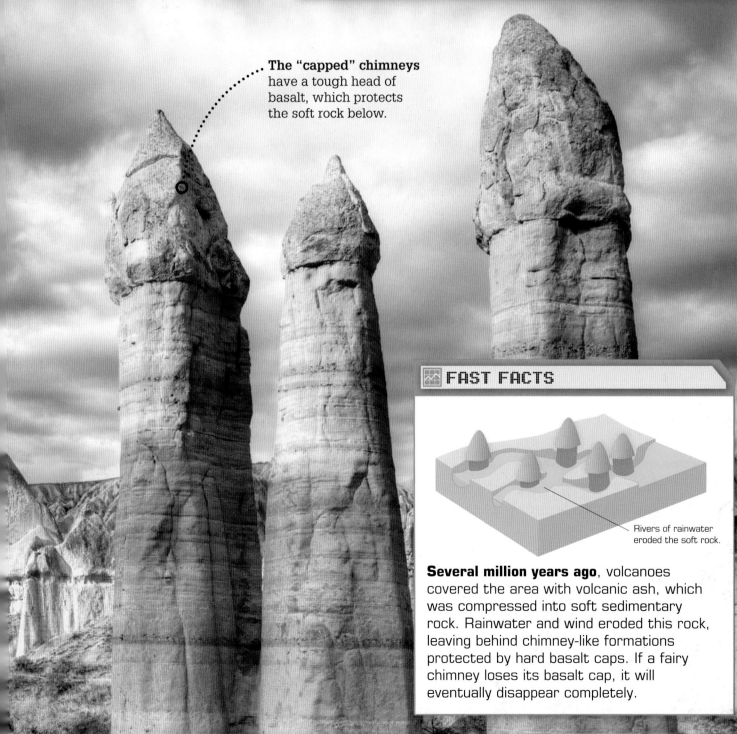

The "capped" chimneys have a tough head of basalt, which protects the soft rock below.

📈 FAST FACTS

Rivers of rainwater eroded the soft rock.

Several million years ago, volcanoes covered the area with volcanic ash, which was compressed into soft sedimentary rock. Rainwater and wind eroded this rock, leaving behind chimney-like formations protected by hard basalt caps. If a fairy chimney loses its basalt cap, it will eventually disappear completely.

Rainbow rocks

There's no need to roll out the red carpet at **Danxia** in **China's Gansu Province**. The jaw-dropping rocky landscape is **naturally red** from a buildup of sandstone over many millions of years, while the **rainbow effect** comes from **colorful mineral deposits**.

LIFE ON MARS

Another red world is Mars. It is called the "Red Planet" because of the dusty surface layer of orange-red iron oxide. Alien life-forms may have lived on Mars three billion years ago when it was warmer and had flowing water.

The name **Danxia means** "rosy clouds" in Chinese.

Danxia's crumpled landscape comes from movement in Earth's crust, combined with wind and rain carving out ravines and pillars in the soft rock.

Covering 154 sq miles (400 sq km), Danxia's rock formations have eroded naturally by wind and rain. This has created today's steep cliffs, solitary peaks, and textured layers. Danxia is the generic term for red sandstone landforms, but kaleidoscopic streaks of yellow, green, and blue from various mineral deposits add to the palette.

FAST FACTS

Over millions of years, sandstone and mineral deposits were compressed into multicolored layers of rock. Movement of the giant plates that form Earth's crust pushed, cut, and folded the layers.

Rain and wind gradually erode the surface, revealing more colored layers.

Bands of sandstone colored by different minerals are laid down.

Plate pushes in

Plate pushes in

The layers fold up as the plates push together.

On the rocks

Wind and water constantly **batter** the planet's rocky regions, sculpting **unusual formations** that must be seen to be believed.

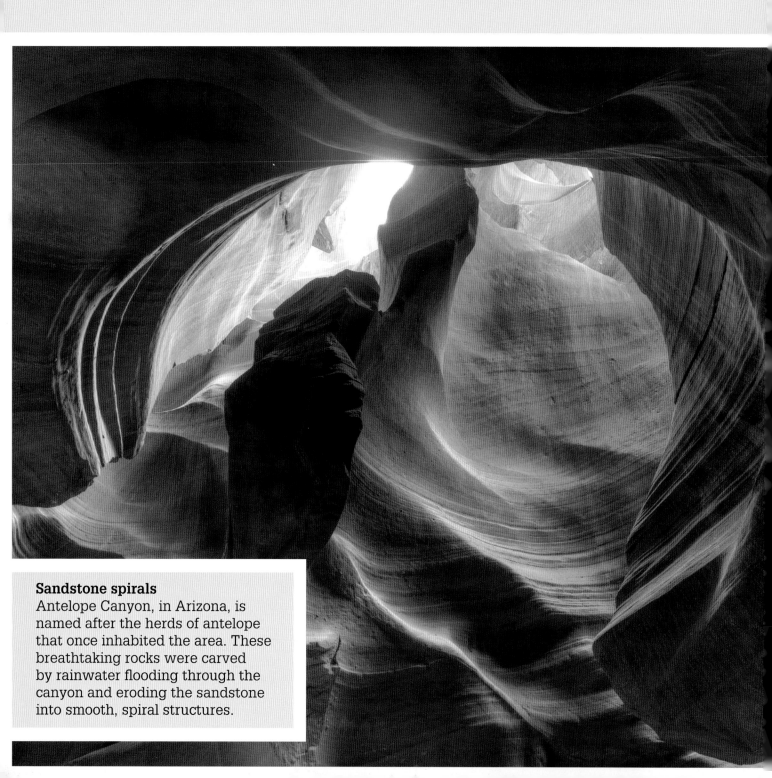

Sandstone spirals
Antelope Canyon, in Arizona, is named after the herds of antelope that once inhabited the area. These breathtaking rocks were carved by rainwater flooding through the canyon and eroding the sandstone into smooth, spiral structures.

Hobgoblin's playground

Little Finland, in Nevada, is named for the fins adorning the desert's red sandstone. The area is also called the Hobgoblin's playground because of its fantastical formations.

Seaside seat

Norway's Kannesteinen rock is the eye-popping result of years of coastal erosion. With its sea view overlooking Vågsøy Island, this distinctive formation is called "the Kanne chair" by locals.

Wipeout wave

The surf's always up at Wave Rock in Hyden, Australia. Stretching 46 ft (14 m) high and reaching 360 ft (110 m) wide, the huge rock resembles a breaking wave and is a sacred spot for Aboriginal locals.

Glorious geyser

Fly Ranch in Nevada's Black Rock Desert is no ordinary geyser. A **faulty well** drilled in the early 1900s caused **geothermally heated water** to burst through surface cracks. Repeated eruptions have left behind **mineral deposits**, forming a multicolored mound.

Each time Fly Ranch Geyser erupts, it releases minerals that have dissolved in the scalding water. These minerals solidify when the water cools, creating an ever-growing mound surrounded by terraced rock pools. Vibrant red and green streaks over the mound are the result of thermophilic (heat-loving) algae thriving in the steamy surroundings.

SPOUTS IN SPACE

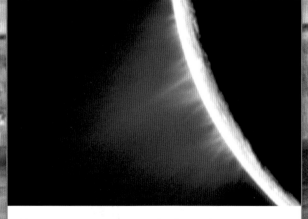

Geysers are not only found on Earth. Saturn's moon Enceladus (above) hosts 101 geysers, while geysers of water vapor were seen spouting on Jupiter's moon Europa in 2013.

Water erupting from the geyser is a piping hot 200°F (93°C) and spills into up to 40 separate pools.

📊 **FAST FACTS**

Geysers occur where underground water comes into contact with hot rocks. Under pressure, the water becomes superheated before reaching boiling point and making its way through cracks in the rock to erupt explosively through a surface vent.

The geyser erupts.

Groundwater soaks through layers of rock.

Water is heated further under pressure and rises to the surface.

Water is heated by contact with hot rocks.

Minerals in the water react with oxygen in the air to create a layer of colorful algae.

The mound continues to grow, adding new layers to its height each year.

The Elephant Foot glacier is on the edge of the vast Greenland ice sheet.

Jumbo glacier

Eye-popping from the air, the **Elephant Foot Glacier** in Greenland is the exact shape of a giant elephant's foot. Made from **compacted snow** over **hundreds of years**, this icy mass has **perfect proportions** and **stunning symmetry**.

The mountains on either side of the glacier stand thousands of feet high, which helps to convey the scale of this icy expanse.

Piedmont glaciers are fan-shaped, and often almost completely symmetrical.

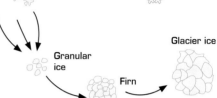

Ground snow

Snowflakes

Glacier ice

Granular ice

Firn

In cold regions, snow does not melt; it piles up in layers. The weight squeezes the snow beneath, forming grains of ice that gradually pack together until they become firn—a middle stage between snow and glacier ice. In a process that can take centuries, the air is squeezed out and the firn turns to dense glacier ice (see p 33).

SILVER-TONGUED GLACIER

The Erebus Ice Tongue in Antarctica is a tongue-like projection extending from the Erebus glacier. Stretching for 7 miles (11 km), parts of the icy tongue have been known to splinter off into the sea, where they become icebergs.

Glaciers are masses of land-based ice that develop at the poles or in areas of high altitude. There are several different types, but all are made from layers of snow and move slowly under their own immense weight. Elephant Foot Glacier is a piedmont glacier, formed when the ice from a steep valley glacier spills over an open plain.

On the hottest days temperatures in the Danakil Depression soar to more than 122°F (50°C).

Sulfur and mineral salt give Danakil its striking colors.

Explosive heat

Few people can stand the **heat** of the **Danakil Depression** in Ethiopia. Active **volcanoes** sizzle inside this desert basin, and sulfur springs emit **choking gases**. No wonder some have called it the **cruelest place** on Earth.

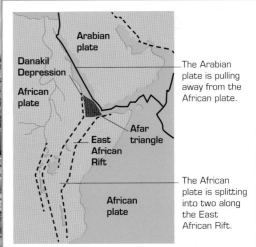

Arabian plate

Danakil Depression

African plate

East African Rift

Afar triangle

African plate

The Arabian plate is pulling away from the African plate.

The African plate is splitting into two along the East African Rift.

The Afar triangle is a vast low area created where Earth's tectonic plates are pulling apart. The huge forces in play as Earth's crust is stretched and thinned causes earthquakes and volcanic eruptions along the plate boundaries. The Danakil Depression, in the north of the triangle, owes its sulfur lakes and active volcanoes to these tectonic forces.

As well as fierce volcanoes and sulfur springs, the Danakil Depression in the Afar triangle is home to acid lakes and occasional earthquakes. It has little to no rainfall and searing temperatures day and night. For centuries local merchants have collected salt from the region's salt flats, and today the most intrepid tourists brave the dangers to marvel at the otherworldly landscape.

EARLIEST ANCESTORS

Fossilized remains of our earliest ancestors have been found in the Afar triangle, not far from the Danakil Depression. In 1974 a team working here found the bones of an early hominid. Dubbed "Lucy" (reconstruction pictured), she is thought to have lived a mind-boggling 3.2 million years ago.

It **rains** almost **every day** of the year on **Mount Roraima.**

Mount Roraima means "big blue-green" in Pemón, a reference to its stunning waterfalls and lush vegetation.

Island in the sky

Imagine a paradise island floating above the clouds and **two billion years** in the making. Welcome to **Mount Roraima** in South America, one of the world's **oldest mountain formations**, with panoramic views across the borders of **Venezuela**, **Brazil**, and **Guyana**.

The cliff tops of this steep plateau stand 1,300 ft (400 m) tall, and the flat summit covers 12 sq miles (31 sq km).

FAST FACTS

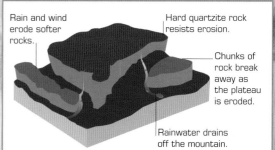

Rain and wind erode softer rocks.

Hard quartzite rock resists erosion.

Chunks of rock break away as the plateau is eroded.

Rainwater drains off the mountain.

Mount Roraima is what is known as a "tabletop" mountain because of its flat top. The flat summit was originally part of a huge sandstone plateau, which fragmented and eroded over millions of years, leaving the mountain towering over the surrounding lowlands.

This unusual mountain inspired Sir Arthur Conan Doyle's book about dinosaurs and humans, *The Lost World*.

TUMBLING TOADS

Mount Roraima is home to a diverse array of animals and plants. The strangest species living here are black pebble toads, said to predate the dinosaurs. Found in 1895, these tiny toads have limited mobility. Unable to swim or hop, they roll themselves into balls and bounce off rocks to escape attackers.

Mount Roraima is the highest peak in the dramatic Pakaraima mountains, considered some of the oldest geological formations ever known. Native Americans believe their gods inhabit these lush mountains, so they call the peaks *tepuis*, which translates in local Pemón as "houses of the gods."

Rainbow spring

One of the world's largest hot springs, **Grand Prismatic Spring** is located in Yellowstone National Park. Explorers gave the spring its name in 1871 after witnessing its incredible **prism of colors**. Measuring 370 ft (113 m) wide and 121 ft (37 m) deep, it releases 560 gallons (2,120 liters) of water a minute.

FIRES OF HELL

Beppu in Japan is home to eight fiery natural springs, known as "hells" (*jigoku*). The Blood Pond Hot Spring is the most famous because of its steaming red waters. This color comes from high levels of iron in the area.

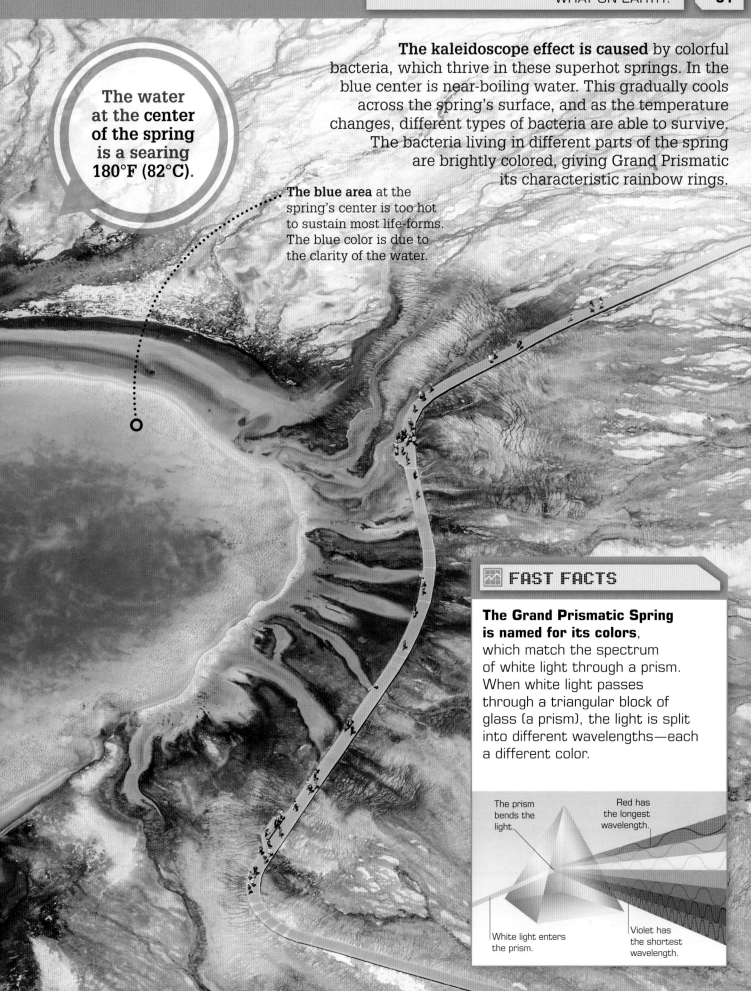

The kaleidoscope effect is caused by colorful bacteria, which thrive in these superhot springs. In the blue center is near-boiling water. This gradually cools across the spring's surface, and as the temperature changes, different types of bacteria are able to survive. The bacteria living in different parts of the spring are brightly colored, giving Grand Prismatic its characteristic rainbow rings.

The water at the center of the spring is a searing 180°F (82°C).

The blue area at the spring's center is too hot to sustain most life-forms. The blue color is due to the clarity of the water.

FAST FACTS

The Grand Prismatic Spring is named for its colors, which match the spectrum of white light through a prism. When white light passes through a triangular block of glass (a prism), the light is split into different wavelengths—each a different color.

The prism bends the light.

Red has the longest wavelength.

White light enters the prism.

Violet has the shortest wavelength.

Ewe with a view

This lone lamb has broken away from the flock to make a gutsy stand on the **Kjeragbolten boulder** in Norway. The confident climber seems oblivious to the **3,228-ft (984-m) drop below.**

Kjeragbolten is the high point of a hiker's paradise on Kjerag mountain in southern Norway. This rock hasn't rolled since 50,000 BCE when it was wedged firmly in place during the last Ice Age. The spot has become the ultimate photo opportunity for tourists, while the area's mountain sheep aren't camera-shy, either.

Adrenaline junkies use the boulder for **BASE jumping**—leaping off, then opening a parachute.

The glacial deposit bridges a gap of 6 ft (2 m) over Lysefjord in the Kjerag mountain range.

The glacier moves downhill very slowly.

Ice

Rocks and stones in the ice erode downward, carving a U-shaped valley.

A fjord is a long, glacier-carved valley flooded by sea water after the glacier has retreated. With their high cliffs, fjords are often spectacularly beautiful.

AERIAL ADRENALINE

Extreme artist Eskil Ronningsbakken, shown here balancing over Trollstigen, Norway, amazes his fans with his aerial antics. He performed a handstand on a stack of chairs on Kjeragbolten, rode a unicycle on a cliff, and pushed a bicycle over a high-flying tightrope.

Deep freeze

Meaning **"glacier of rivers,"** Vatnajökull is the **largest glacier** in Europe, covering almost 10 percent of Iceland. Underneath the ice is a **frozen world** called the Crystal Caves, a **hidden labyrinth** of blue chambers and tunnels that change with the seasons.

The ice is 3,300 ft (1,000 m) deep at its thickest point.

ADVANCING ICE

Stretching for 19 miles (30 km), Perito Moreno in Argentina is an unusual glacier because it is advancing, rather than shrinking. Heavy chunks of ice break off regularly, dropping into the shimmering waters of Lake Argentino.

In the summer sunshine the surface of Vatnajökull's thick glacial ice melts, and the resulting water flows into holes and cracks on the surface. Underneath the glacier, rivers of this meltwater cut through the ancient glacier ice, leaving behind magnificent glacial caves. Each year the caves appear in different places—local guides scout their location and take tourists to those that are safe to visit.

FAST FACTS

Seven colors make up the white light that we see.

Only the blue light is reflected.

Dense glacier ice absorbs most of the colors.

Why is the ice blue? Thick, dense glacier ice doesn't contain air bubbles, which would reflect lots of light and make the ice appear white. Rather, the ice absorbs most of the colors that make up white light and reflects only the blue—which is what you see.

The ice comprising the Vatnajökull glacier is about 1,000 years old.

Cool caves

Hidden away deep inside **Earth's crust** is a magical **subterranean world** of caverns, such as these stunning examples.

Psychedelic salt mine
A former salt mine in Yekaterinburg, Russia, is now one of the world's most colorful caves. More than 650 ft (200 m) underground, its patterned rainbow walls are caused by the mineral carnallite swirling in layers through the rock.

Crystal caves

Only discovered in 2000, the Cave of the Crystals in Mexico is part of the Naica Mine and is home to the largest crystals in the world. Some of the giant selenite crystals it contains have grown to more than 33 ft (10 m) in length.

Marble marvels

Crashing waves have eroded and sculpted Patagonia's Marble Caves. One of the caves is called the Marble Cathedral, after its distinctive sweeping arches. Eye-catching reflections of the shimmering blue water dance across white marble ceilings.

Stone forest

Like an enchanted forest that's been turned to stone, **Grand Tsingy** in Madagascar is a somber scene of **spiky, tree-like rocks**. The world's largest stone forest was carved by **tropical rain** in a process that lasted millions of years.

Tsingy de Bemaraha covers a vast 230 sq miles (600 sq km).

The canyon walls are up to 328 m (100 ft) tall.

The razor-sharp, vertical stones of Grand Tsingy challenge even the most experienced rock climbers.

EXTREME LIVING

A surprising number of species call Tsingy de Bemaraha national park their home. More than 100 types of bird, at least 30 types of reptile, and 11 types of lemur, including the Decken's sifaka (above), live here. Many are found nowhere else in the world.

Meaning "where one cannot walk," Grand Tsingy is an isolated wilderness in Madagascar's Tsingy de Bemaraha national park. Its limestone rock has been eroded into a grid-like pattern of dead-straight canyons called grikes, topped with dangerously craggy spears. Though the entire area appears gray rather than green, plant life flourishes between the peaks.

FAST FACTS

Groundwater flowing along fracture lines in the rock cut caves in the limestone of Grand Tsingy, while monsoon rains eroded the surface.

Over millions of years the water continued to erode the caves, causing them to expand and merge into deep, narrow underground caverns.

The cave ceilings then collapsed, exposing the network of towering canyons we see today, topped with sharp peaks carved by surface erosion.

Red alert!

Tanzania's Lake Natron has a **killer reputation.** Said to **turn local wildlife to stone**, its bright red waters certainly seem to **signal danger**. But in fact, the concentration of harmful chemicals in this **alkaline lake** supports a rich ecosystem.

THRIVING FLAMINGOS

Despite the dangers, about 2.5 million lesser flamingos nest on Lake Natron, making it one of the largest breeding grounds for this African species. They build their nests on small islands that form in the lake during the dry season, and feed on the plentiful algae inhabiting the waters.

Alkali salt deposits have formed a crisscross pattern on the lake.

The blood-red color is caused by microorganisms that thrive in the salty waters.

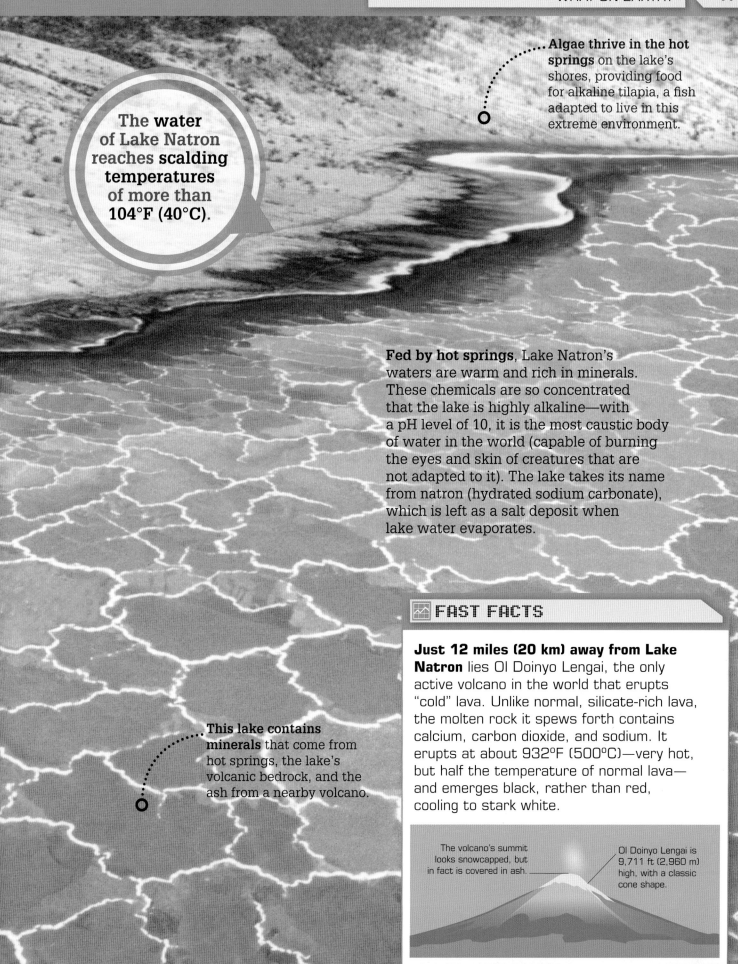

Algae thrive in the hot springs on the lake's shores, providing food for alkaline tilapia, a fish adapted to live in this extreme environment.

The **water** of Lake Natron reaches **scalding temperatures** of more than 104°F (40°C).

Fed by hot springs, Lake Natron's waters are warm and rich in minerals. These chemicals are so concentrated that the lake is highly alkaline—with a pH level of 10, it is the most caustic body of water in the world (capable of burning the eyes and skin of creatures that are not adapted to it). The lake takes its name from natron (hydrated sodium carbonate), which is left as a salt deposit when lake water evaporates.

This lake contains minerals that come from hot springs, the lake's volcanic bedrock, and the ash from a nearby volcano.

FAST FACTS

Just 12 miles (20 km) away from Lake Natron lies Ol Doinyo Lengai, the only active volcano in the world that erupts "cold" lava. Unlike normal, silicate-rich lava, the molten rock it spews forth contains calcium, carbon dioxide, and sodium. It erupts at about 932°F (500°C)—very hot, but half the temperature of normal lava—and emerges black, rather than red, cooling to stark white.

The volcano's summit looks snowcapped, but in fact is covered in ash.

Ol Doinyo Lengai is 9,711 ft (2,960 m) high, with a classic cone shape.

Giant's Causeway

Hailed as the **eighth wonder of the world**, the Giant's Causeway on the north coast of Northern Ireland consists of a pathway of about **40,000** interlocking **basalt columns**. A **famous legend** explains its creation, but it really resulted from a **volcanic eruption**.

The earliest account of the Causeway's existence dates from 1693.

MYSTERY MEN

Chalk outlines of giant human figures seen on England's landscape date back to the Iron Age. Locals living near the Long Man of Wilmington (above) in East Sussex and the Cerne Abbas Giant in Dorset traditionally associated them with luck and fertility.

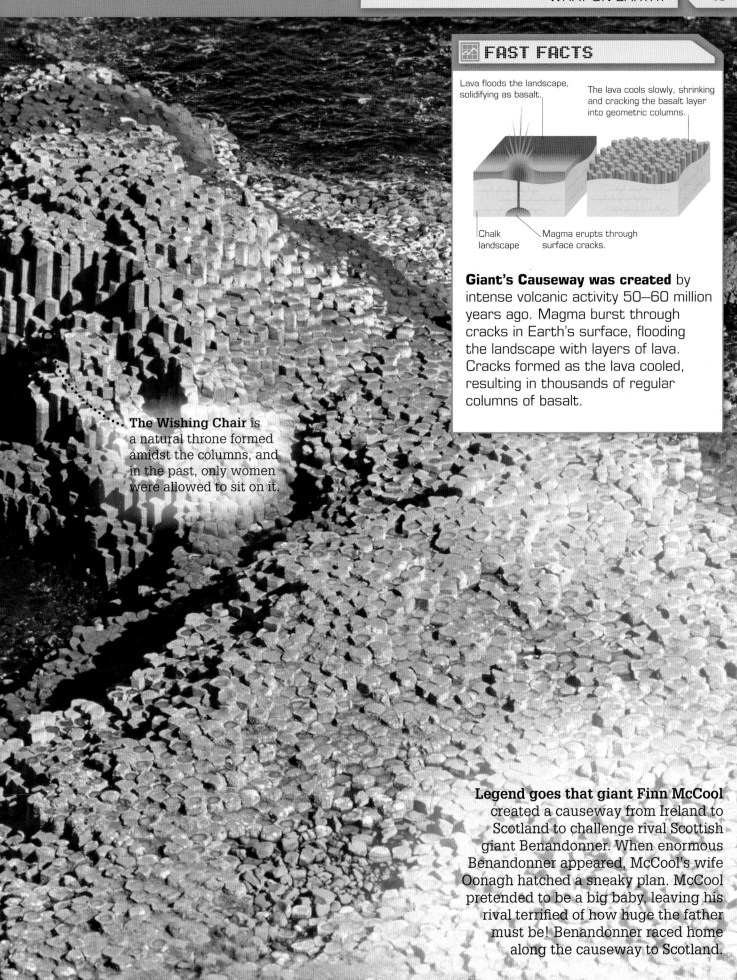

📊 **FAST FACTS**

Lava floods the landscape, solidifying as basalt.

The lava cools slowly, shrinking and cracking the basalt layer into geometric columns.

Chalk landscape

Magma erupts through surface cracks.

Giant's Causeway was created by intense volcanic activity 50–60 million years ago. Magma burst through cracks in Earth's surface, flooding the landscape with layers of lava. Cracks formed as the lava cooled, resulting in thousands of regular columns of basalt.

The Wishing Chair is a natural throne formed amidst the columns, and in the past, only women were allowed to sit on it.

Legend goes that giant Finn McCool created a causeway from Ireland to Scotland to challenge rival Scottish giant Benandonner. When enormous Benandonner appeared, McCool's wife Oonagh hatched a sneaky plan. McCool pretended to be a big baby, leaving his rival terrified of how huge the father must be! Benandonner raced home along the causeway to Scotland.

Human wonders

There is no limit to imagination. People have always made their mark on the world, from ancient innovations and contemporary constructions to death-defying endeavors and thrill-seeking stunts. All around the planet different cultures enrich their environments, sometimes in the most unexpected ways.

The world's largest ice festival has been held annually at Harbin in northeastern China since 1985. Packed with sculptures, the "Ice City" is best seen at night when its ice castles and lanterns are illuminated.

Desert drawings

Aircraft pilots flying over Peru's **Nazca desert** in the 1930s were amazed to see huge drawings **scratched into the landscape**. These **geoglyphs** are called **Nazca lines**, after the ancient Nazcas who made them, and they are a fascinating tribute to a **lost people**.

The monkey has three toes on each foot, four fingers on one hand, and five on the other. Some historians think the number of digits may have had a hidden meaning.

This geoglyph represents a monkey and measures 180 ft (55 m) long.

📈 FAST FACTS

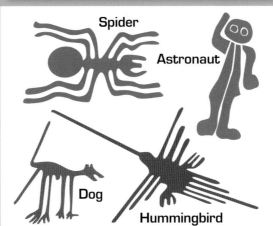

Spider

Astronaut

Dog

Hummingbird

The mysterious lines are found on a coastal plain between two river valleys. There are hundreds of individual designs, and many more shapes and straight lines. They were created over several centuries, with some newer geoglyphs overlapping or obscuring older ones. In 2014 previously unknown geoglyphs were uncovered by a sandstorm.

The geoglyphs cover a vast area of about 174 sq miles (450 sq km).

Crafted between 500 BCE and 500 CE, the Nazca lines include images of animals, birds, and human-like figures. The reason for their construction remains uncertain. Some historians believe the lines were art created for the gods to enjoy, while others speculate that they were maps of underground water sources or an early form of calendar.

The huge lines were created by removing the dark top layer of gravel to reveal the lighter-colored earth underneath.

NAZCA WORSHIP

The Nazca people believed that worshipping the gods was key to survival. Their expertly crafted pottery features depictions of their gods, as well as nature spirits and mythical creatures. The Nazca had no writing system, so painting pots would have been one way of communicating their beliefs.

Clay corps

A **chance discovery** of a hidden pit in Xian, China, led to an incredible find— nearly **8,000 life-size soldiers** sculpted **2,200 years ago**. Called the **Terracotta army**, these clay figures were crafted to protect the tomb of China's **First Emperor**, Qin Shi Huang.

Statues were modeled in clay and originally painted in bright colors.

EXTENSIVE EXCAVATIONS

Four pits were found, but the last was empty, suggesting the mausoleum was incomplete when the emperor died. Many warriors lay in pieces and were painstakingly restored. They had been preserved due to the consistent temperature from burial until excavation.

FAST FACTS

One of the warriors' huge crossbows could fire an arrow the length of seven and a half soccer fields.

The warriors' weapons were real, but never used in battle. Thousands of bronze spears, battle-axes, crossbows, and arrowheads have been uncovered in great condition. One crossbow found was about 5 ft (1.5 m) long, and was capable of firing an arrow as far as 2,600 ft (792 m).

Each warrior is unique, with its own hairstyle, facial features, and expression.

The emperor's tomb lies 0.93 miles (1.5 km) away at Mount Li and remains undisturbed.

Attention to detail is remarkable—even shoe soles, where visible, have their own intricate patterns.

In 1974 Chinese farmers were digging a well when they uncovered the pit housing the Terracotta army. Lined up according to rank, there are archers, charioteers, officers, generals, and horsemen. A production-line approach was used to make each warrior, with every body part crafted separately before the figure was fully assembled at the end.

Happy endings

Funerals in the West African country of Ghana are **upbeat gatherings**. Innovative coffins **celebrate** the deceased's work or interests.

Flight of fancy
Two brothers created this wooden aircraft coffin for their grandmother, who had never been in a plane but dreamed of flying.

Snap-happy
Many coffins reflect the deceased's career, such as this camera-shaped coffin for a photographer.

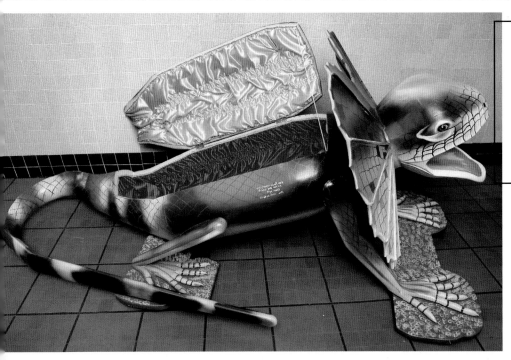

Coffin art
Examples of the handcrafted, ornately decorated caskets have been displayed all over the world. This lizard coffin was created for an exhibition in Melbourne, Australia.

Final fizz
No need to guess the deceased's drink of choice. Favorite foods can also be reflected in the shape of a coffin.

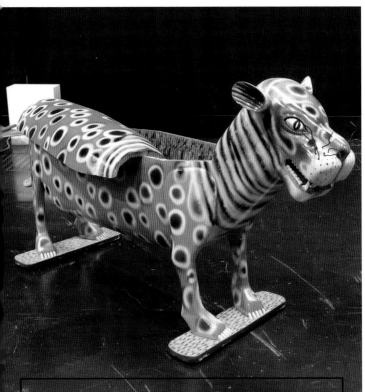

Luxury at a price
Fantasy coffins offer lavishly lined interiors, as this open leopard coffin shows, and cost about $750 each. This is equivalent to about a year's wages, so usually only the wealthier Ghanaians can afford them.

Secret city

Turkey's ancient underground caves of **Cappadocia** were once **inhabited cities**. Steep, hollowed hillsides mask a **secret subterranean world**.

Derinkuyu is about 279 ft (85 m) deep and carved out of **volcanic rock**.

Derinkuyu had **11 floors** and a network of random tunnels to deter would-be invaders.

The deepest of Cappadocia's underground cities, Derinkuyu had sleeping quarters, communal rooms, bathrooms, cooking pits, wells, ventilation shafts, churches, and stables for animals. Historians believe this was the hiding place for early Christians trying to flee persecution from the Roman empire. At its peak, the city may have housed up to 20,000 people.

📊 FACT FACTS

One of about 40 cities, Derinkuyu had at least 600 entrances, hidden in the courtyards of houses above ground. The city's inhabitants used heavy circular stone doors to block tunnels from the inside in the event of an attack.

The stone was rolled into the narrow passage and wedged from behind to block attackers.

DOWN UNDER

Sweltering summer temperatures made life difficult for locals in the Australian opal mining town of Coober Pedy—so, in 1915, they decided to retreat underground. About half of the town's 4,000 inhabitants still live underground in homes known as "dugouts."

Mysterious moai

Standing head and shoulders above the volcanic land of **Easter Island** are moai—huge human heads carved from rock more than **500 years** ago. Created by the **ancient Polynesians**, the sculptures are still **sacred** to today's islanders.

Each moai has been carved out of soft volcanic rock.

FAMOUS FACES

Mount Rushmore, in South Dakota, is famous for its cliff carvings of four US Presidents— George Washington, Thomas Jefferson, Theodore Roosevelt, and Abraham Lincoln. From 1927 until the carvings' completion in 1941, about 400 people worked on the faces.

Easter Island is 1,100 miles (1,700 km) away from its nearest island neighbor.

The average height of a moai is 13 ft (4 m) and the average weight is 14 tons.

The moai are testament to the extraordinary capabilities of the ancient Polynesians because they were difficult to construct and tough to transport around Easter Island. There are 887 statues, all of them male. Most experts believe the moai were meant to honor the spirits of deceased ancestors, existing chiefs, or others special to the Polynesians, but nothing has been proven.

FAST FACTS

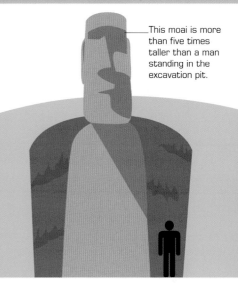

This moai is more than five times taller than a man standing in the excavation pit.

A large part of each moai is unseen because it is buried underground. The height of the tallest statue ever erected on Easter Island is about 33 ft (10 m).

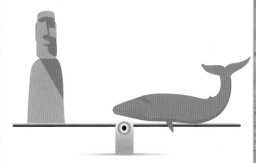

The biggest statue, nicknamed "El Gigante," was found in a quarry. This mega moai is 72 ft (22 m) tall and weighs about 180 tons—as much as a large blue whale.

Top of the tree

Making their homes in the treetops of Papua, Indonesian New Guinea, the Korowai people are **traditional hunter-gatherers** who use the rain forest's resources to **craft their tree houses.** This remote location meant the tribe's existence was **secret** until recently.

Towering above the ground, each house has a large Banyan tree at its center. Branches and leaves are bound with rattan to make floors and walls. Families of up to 12 people can inhabit one house. Fire is a big concern, so hearths are designed with cut-away floor sections to stop flames from spreading.

There are fewer than 3,000 Korowai people now living on the island of New Guinea.

A makeshift ladder is hung from the bottom of each tree house to gain entry.

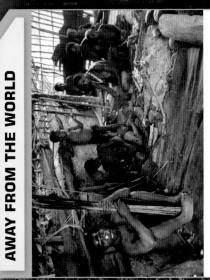

AWAY FROM THE WORLD

The Korowai lived in complete isolation from the rest of the world until 1974, when Dutch missionaries discovered them. They are said to be one of the last active tribes of cannibals (people who eat one another).

FAST FACTS

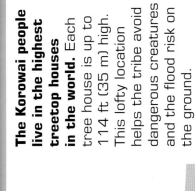

The Korowai people live in the highest treetop houses in the world. Each tree house is up to 114 ft (35 m) high. This lofty location helps the tribe avoid dangerous creatures and the flood risk on the ground.

Deep breath

The depths some people dive will **take your breath away**. From the earliest times, people have taken the plunge, but today **free diving** (diving without breathing equipment) is an **extreme sport** that pushes the human body to its **absolute limit**. Participants dive the depths on just one **deep breath**.

FREE DIVING FOR FOOD

The Bajau people of Borneo are real water babies. Their houses stand on stilts in the sea, and they free dive in search of fish to eat. The best Bajau free divers can stay submerged on a single breath for up to five minutes, diving to the bottom of the reef 66 ft (20 m) below.

As the depth increases, so does the amount of water pressing down on free diver Pierre Frolla from above. Free divers must learn to cope with the extreme conditions.

At a depth of 328 ft (100 m) water pressure compresses human lungs to the size of fists.

This wreck of an aircraft is in the Bahamas.

FAST FACTS

Constant weight without fins world record: 331 ft (101 m)

Constant weight with fins world record: 419 ft (128 m)

No limits world record: 702 ft (214 m)

Competitive free diving has different disciplines depending on what equipment the diver uses. "No limits" free diving involves using a weight and cable to descend very quickly. "Constant weight" free divers descend and ascend under their own power. They can use a weight to help them descend, but must return to the surface with the same weight.

Holding their breath for minutes at a time, free divers plunge to depths of more than 328 ft (100 m). Divers train themselves for the challenge mentally and physically, but in some ways the human body is hardwired to undertake this amazing aquatic activity. When submerged in cold water, the heart rate slows to conserve oxygen. The blood moves away from the arms and legs to protect the vital organs.

Wet and **wild**

Crossing the raging rapids of Asia's **Mekong River** on a precarious rope bridge is part of the daily routine for **local Lao fishermen**. However high the water, they must navigate the **dangerous currents** to secure a top spot and net a big catch.

More than **1,300 species of fish inhabit the Mekong River.**

SCHOOL'S OUT

The school run is a challenge in some parts of the world. These pupils must walk for two hours each day to attend their school in the mountains of Bijie, Guizhou Province, China. As well as passing through narrow tunnels in the rock, they must travel this treacherous cliff path, which is only 1 ft 7 in (0.5 m) wide.

With swirling rapids and crashing waterfalls, the Mekong River is unpredictable, experiencing huge fluctuations in flow throughout the year. But the river's wild waters contain a large variety of fish, making fishing the most common occupation for Mekong's riverside dwellers. This fisherman is risking a treacherous trip over a makeshift bridge to reach a prime fishing spot.

This precarious tightrope was built by a local fisherman using bits of rope and old cable.

The Chinese name for Mekong translates as "turbulent river," while the Thai and Lao name means "mother water." The Vietnamese call it "nine dragons" after the delta's many tributaries.

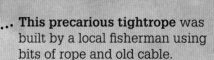

📈 FAST FACTS

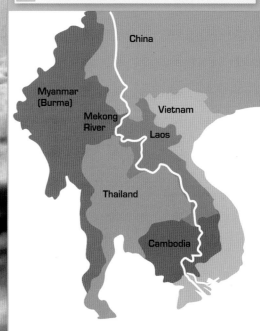

China

Myanmar (Burma)

Mekong River

Vietnam

Laos

Thailand

Cambodia

Stretching about 3,000 miles (4,800 km), the Mekong is the world's 12th longest river. It flows through China, Myanmar, Thailand, Laos, Cambodia, and Vietnam.

Honey hunters

The **Gurung tribesmen** of Nepal make a living by collecting honeycomb from **gravity-defying** Himalayan cliffs. They put themselves in the **stickiest** of situations, dangling from rope ladders to access the sweet treat.

Blisters and bee stings are common complaints, but honey hunting can be fatal.

RISKY BUSINESS

Honey hunters in the Sundarbans forests of Bangladesh run the risk of tiger attacks. They light fires beside cliffs to smoke the bees out, but many hunters are injured or killed when the big cats come to investigate.

Balancing precariously up to 300 ft (90 m) above the ground, honey hunters use thick smoke to sedate huge swarms of angry bees. This tradition has been going on for thousands of years. Some of the honey is shared among the villagers to make tea, and the rest is sold.

Honey hunters use "tangos"—tools adapted from bamboo sticks—to cut the honey from the cliff face.

FAST FACTS

Measuring up to 1⅛ in (3 cm) in length, the Himalayan honey bee (*Apis laboriosa*) is the largest honey bee in the world. It lives at high altitude and builds its large, precarious nests on the sides of vertical cliffs.

The Western honey bee is just ½ in (1.2 cm) long.

Himalayan honey bee

Tower of strength

Since the 18th century a **fascinating festival** has taken place in Spain's Catalonia region. Here, **human tower building** is a competitive sport, in which **courageous castellers** (builders) attempt to create a formation that stands head and shoulders above the rest.

At this twice-yearly arena event, teams of castellers work together to build the most impressive human towers as quickly as possible. The last member in position raises one hand with four fingers outstretched to represent the Catalan flag. The best score goes to the most intricate tower to be assembled and dismantled successfully.

Children climb up to form the higher levels.

Dismounting is the hardest part, so a medical crew must be standing by.

FAST FACTS

The top section, or *pom*, must be assembled rapidly.

The main section of the tower is called the trunk, or *tronc*.

The solid base, or *pinya*, provides support and cushioning if the tower collapses.

The tallest castell on record was 10 tiers high, with three people at each level. It was built by local castellers at the annual Vilafranca festival in Catalonia. More than 500 people provided support at the base of the tower.

DOUBLE CELEBRATION

Everyone loves a party! Inhabitants of the town of Bérchules in Spain celebrate the new year twice a year. A power outage on December 31, 1994, ruined the usual festivities, so they had another New Year's Eve party in August. The tradition continues to this day.

Food fight festival

Tomatoes are weapons of war at the annual **La Tomatina**, the messiest day on Spain's festival calendar. This **celebratory fruit-fest** is now the world's biggest food fight. Armed with an endless supply of **squashed tomatoes,** thousands of participants **prepare for pelting**!

This crowd is restricted to 20,000 people—double the town's usual population. In the past, 50,000 people crammed into Buñol for the festival.

MELON MADNESS

The fruit of choice at the Chinchilla Festival in Australia is the watermelon. Taking center stage every other February, watermelons are celebrated in a number of activities, with melon skiing (above), melon tossing, and pip spitting all on the menu.

Participants are pulped with overripe tomatoes, transforming the crowd into a soupy red mess.

FAST FACTS

An astonishing 240,000 lb (110,000 kg) of tomatoes are thrown at the festival—the weight of a small blue whale.

Tomato juice is acidic. It acts as a natural cleaning fluid on the streets of Buñol.

Since 1945 the town of Buñol has become a crimson tide of tomatoes on the last Wednesday of August, though no one knows why the event started. A water cannon fires and battle begins. Tomatoes are thrown in all directions for an hour before the lengthy cleanup operation gets underway.

Festival fun

Whether steeped in **ancient tradition** and **religious custom**, or just a good excuse to have fun, festivals are **special days**. They give communities the chance to congregate and **celebrate together**.

Songkran squirters
Thailand's traditional New Year gets underway with the Songkran water festival. Elephants spray water, children squirt pistols, and water-filled buckets drench passersby. This supersized water fight marks the wet season starting in April.

Big fish festival
Since 1934 the Argungu Fishing Festival has welcomed an influx of fishermen to the Matan Fada River in the Nigerian state of Kebbi. Brandishing nets and gourds, the person who catches the biggest fish within an hour wins money and a bus!

Remarkable radishes
The Night of the Radishes on December 23 sees Oaxaca City in Mexico grind to a halt. A radish-carving competition is held, with the fruits— or rather, vegetables—of participants' labor shown to an audience of thousands.

Snow sculptures

Since 1950 the world's biggest annual **celebration of snow** has caused flurries of excitement at **Sapporo** in Japan. More than **2.4 million visitors** descend on the city to wonder at the **snow sculptures** and toast the winner of the coolest competition around.

The amount of snow used at the Sapporo festival is more than 36,000 tons.

SNOWY SANCTUARY

The Hôtel de Glace in Quebec, Canada, is a dream destination for snow bunnies. The hotel is crafted almost entirely from snow and ice, offering visitors an ice chapel for wedding ceremonies, an ice slide, and an ice bar.

Fairytale castles and giant figures are among the sculptures on display.

At the Sapporo Snow Festival, held every February, teams from around the world compete to develop the most imaginative and incredible snow sculptures. What began on a small scale, with school students displaying amateur efforts at the city's Odori Park, has grown to become one of the largest global events on the winter calendar, featuring hundreds of sculptures.

The largest snow sculptures can reach 50 ft (15 m) tall and 80 ft (24 m) wide.

FAST FACTS

Sculpting starts with trucks transporting snow to the site, where bulldozers pack it into a firm base.

A frame is packed with more snow to form a solid block. The wooden boards are removed and carving begins.

The frame is removed for the final details. Teams have just 20 hours from start to finish to create their art.

Plane spotter's
paradise

The **jet blast** from the aircraft could **knock over or even kill a person** in its path.

One of the Caribbean's busiest airports, Princess Juliana International on Saint Martin island has unintentionally become a tourist attraction due to its low-flying aircraft. Saint Martin is the smallest island to be split between two nations. Holland and France share the idyllic isle, with Maho Beach on the Dutch side.

A ROUND ON THE RUNWAY

Kantarat's 18-hole golf course is tightly sandwiched between two runways of Thailand's Don Mueang Airport. Traffic signals help golf carts to cruise between holes safely.

Maho Beach is no peaceful paradise. Its blue skies are overshadowed by **low-flying jets**, while the crashing Caribbean surf is drowned out by **roaring engines**. With the runway just 20 ft (6 m) from the sand, thrill seekers and plane spotters can experience **extreme encounters** with aircraft every single day.

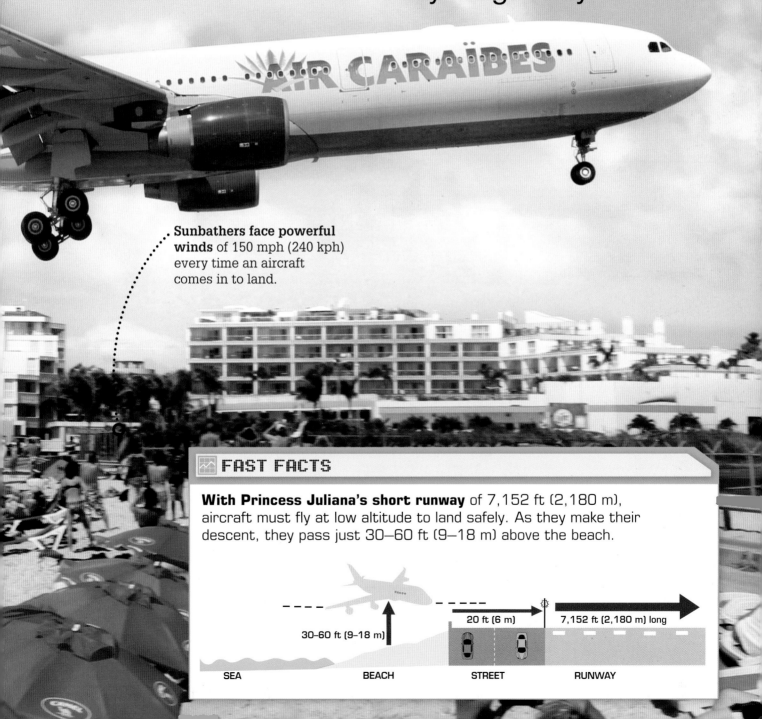

Sunbathers face powerful winds of 150 mph (240 kph) every time an aircraft comes in to land.

FAST FACTS

With Princess Juliana's short runway of 7,152 ft (2,180 m), aircraft must fly at low altitude to land safely. As they make their descent, they pass just 30–60 ft (9–18 m) above the beach.

30–60 ft (9–18 m)

20 ft (6 m)

7,152 ft (2,180 m) long

SEA   BEACH   STREET   RUNWAY

Leap of faith

Before bungee jumping, there was a scarier sport. A **daredevil diving ritual** called Naghol has been a tradition for centuries on **Pentecost Island** in the South Pacific. Local men risk life and limb to throw themselves from **dizzying heights** with only a **jungle vine** around their ankles.

Land diving was first performed from treetops, but now fragile towers have been constructed. Before the jump, men and women chant and dance until one man climbs the tower, where vines are attached to his ankles. The diver jumps headfirst, dropping to the ground at high speed. Locals believe that the braver the divers are, the more bountiful the yam harvest will be.

Land diving takes place after the wet season, so that the vines will be water-logged to maximize their elasticity and strength.

Land diving is a rite of passage for the island's young men.

The divers leap from platforms that may be more than 65 ft (20 m) off the ground.

FAST FACTS

One of the world's highest bungee jumps is the Macau Tower in China. Sending adrenaline junkies spiraling down from a 764-ft (233-m) platform on the tower's outer rim, there is a six-second freefall before the elastic bounces back. The top height for a Naghol diving tower is 130 ft (40 m)—you'd have to stack six end to end to match the Macau bungee.

Macau Tower

Naghol diving towers

LUCKY ESCAPE

The land diving ritual stems from a legend of an unhappy marriage, in which a woman was running through the jungle desperate to escape her pesky husband. She climbed a tree with him hot on her heels, tied a vine to her ankle, and jumped. She landed safely, but her husband did not secure himself and did not survive the jump.

Street View has also gone **underwater** to capture the **Great Barrier Reef**.

The Street View Trekker camera can also be worn as a backpack, allowing people to photograph hard-to-reach places.

Raffia and her guide trekked the desert at sunrise to capture the best lighting for their shots.

TIMING IS EVERYTHING

When the Street View car cameras have been in the right place at the right time, they have caught rainbows (above), lightning strikes, and butterflies landing on their lenses. But when the timing goes wrong, birds narrowly miss crashing into cameras, or their droppings seriously spoil the view!

FAST FACTS

Street View covers over 5 million miles (8 million km) of road across 39 countries, and continues to add more images. In addition to cities and towns, the project has captured panoramas of iconic sites such as the pyramids of Giza and Everest Base Camp.

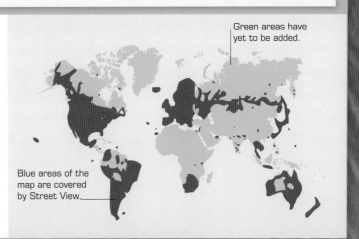

Green areas have yet to be added.

Blue areas of the map are covered by Street View.

Google Maps has been providing Google Street View online since 2007. The panoramic views it provides are made of still photographs, often captured by a car-mounted camera. But the Liwa Desert in the United Arab Emirates is not the average street view. These sprawling dunes needed a unique photographer, and an animal already adapted to desert life was the obvious choice.

Camel's camera

Traditionally called "ships of the desert," camels are now vessels for photographing the world. Ten-year-old Raffia captured the **Liwa Desert** on a **camera attached to her hump**, becoming the first creature to assist Google in its quest to **map our planet**.

Daredevil climber

Spider-Man **scaling skyscrapers** is the stuff of superhero stories. But one Frenchman has **brought comic strips to life** with a series of incredible climbs. His **amazing antics** have led to both awards and arrests around the world.

Alain Robert has spent so long as a **free climber** he can **no longer** fully straighten his fingers.

Free solo climber Alain Robert is seen here on his way up the Abu Dhabi Investment Authority (ADIA) Building, United Arab Emirates, in 2007. The skyscraper is 607 ft (185 m) high.

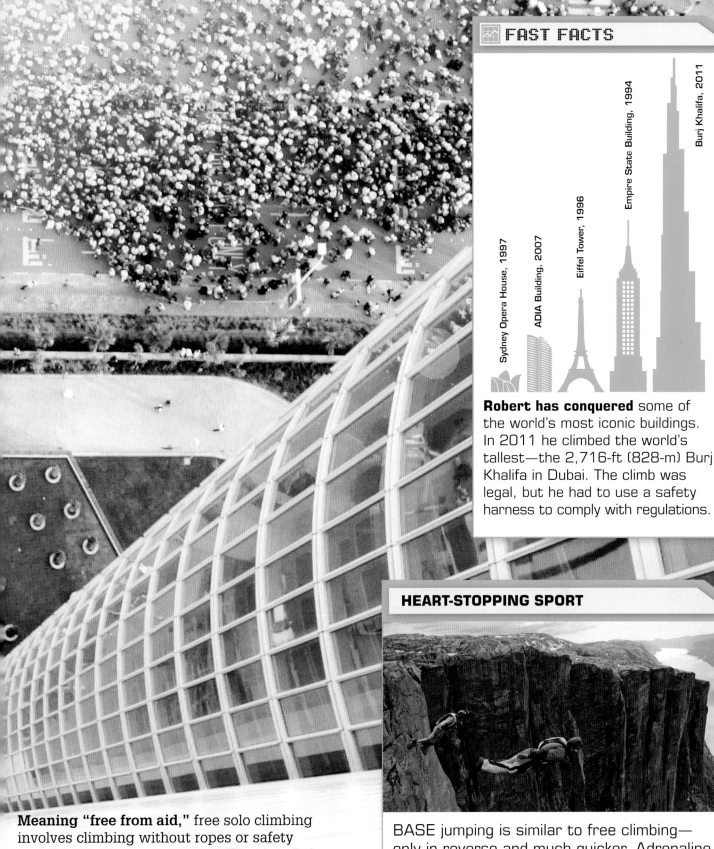

Sydney Opera House, 1997

ADIA Building, 2007

Eiffel Tower, 1996

Empire State Building, 1994

Burj Khalifa, 2011

Robert has conquered some of the world's most iconic buildings. In 2011 he climbed the world's tallest—the 2,716-ft (828-m) Burj Khalifa in Dubai. The climb was legal, but he had to use a safety harness to comply with regulations.

HEART-STOPPING SPORT

Meaning "free from aid," free solo climbing involves climbing without ropes or safety equipment. Climber extraordinaire Alain Robert has reached the summit of the world's tallest buildings, often using just a pair of climbing shoes and his bare hands. Some of his stunts have been authorized, but he has also been arrested many times for scaling buildings without permission.

BASE jumping is similar to free climbing—only in reverse and much quicker. Adrenaline enthusiasts leap from a fixed point, such as a cliff or building. They free-fall before opening a parachute just in the nick of time to land safely.

At the top of their **game**

This pair of aces were hitting high during their breathtaking **tennis match** on the **helipad of a seven-star hotel** in Dubai. Switzerland's Roger Federer played the USA's Andre Agassi in a friendly game on the **world's highest court** in 2005.

Federer and Agassi were in training for the Dubai Duty Free Men's Championship when they gave this sky-high court a try.

GAMES WITH ALTITUDE

In 2007, FIFA (soccer's governing body) banned international soccer matches at high altitude. Playing at more than 8,200 ft (2,500 m) above sea level can be damaging to health. The thinner air gives an advantage to players used to such conditions. This field in Switzerland is at 6,560 ft (2,000 m).

It is now possible to get married on the Burj Al Arab helipad—at vast expense.

FAST FACTS

The diameter of the helipad is just 79 ft (24 m).

Donut rings

An average Formula One car is 15 ft (4.5 m) long.

The Burj Al Arab helipad has also been home to other sports stunts. Formula One driver David Coulthard performed donuts in a race car in 2013—no easy feat in such a small space—and golfers Rory McIlroy and Tiger Woods have teed off from there.

The luxurious Burj Al Arab stands 1,053 ft (321 m) tall on a specially built island. Both players had the advantage when they saw the views of Dubai from the hotel's helipad, 692 ft (211 m) up. They smashed a few balls over the edge into the sea, but no one was eager to go retrieve them!

Basket Building

Although it looks like the food basket from a giants' picnic, this **basket-shaped building** is open for business. Completed in 1997, the award-winning **architectural achievement** in Ohio is the brainchild of basket entrepreneur Dave Longaberger.

The building measures 192 ft (58 m) by 126 ft (38 m) at its base and 208 ft (63 m) by 142 ft (43 m) at the roof.

ADVERTISER'S DREAM

The USA has lots of buildings designed to showcase the products on sale inside. Twistee Treat's ice cream outlets are shaped like cones, Kansas City Library's parking lot (above) resembles a bookshelf, and Furnitureland in North Carolina looks like a chest of drawers.

Founder of the Longaberger Company
Dave Longaberger dreamed up the idea to house his offices inside the world's biggest basket. The building is a scaled-up version of the handcrafted maple wood baskets manufactured and distributed by Longaberger. Inside the lavish seven-story building in Newark, Ohio, are marble floors, cherry woodwork, and a sweeping staircase.

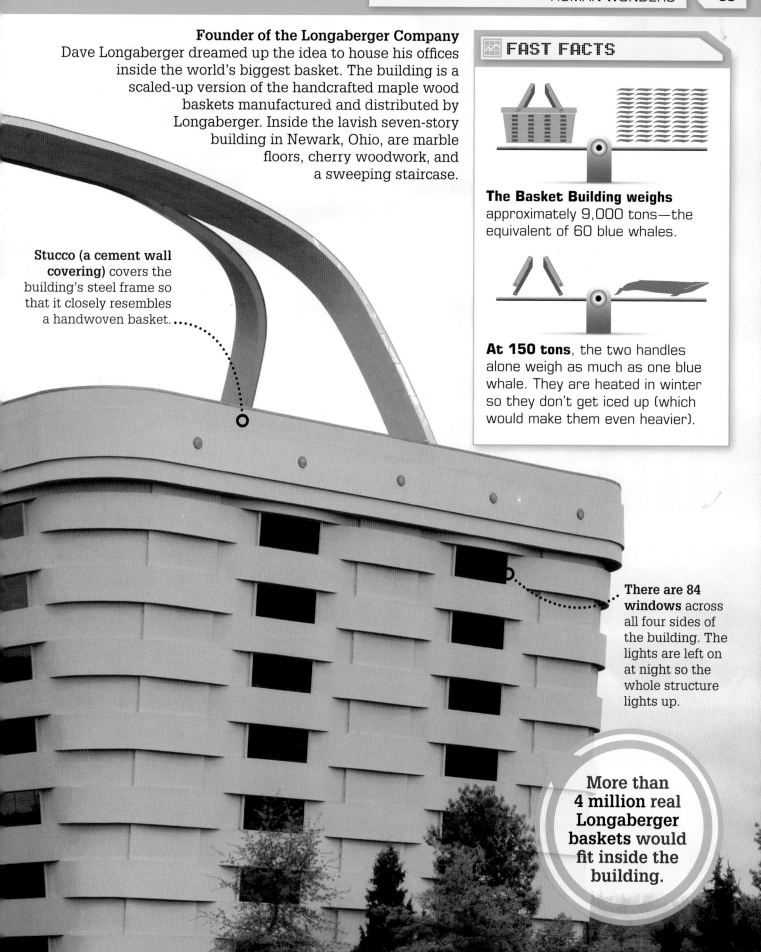

Stucco (a cement wall covering) covers the building's steel frame so that it closely resembles a handwoven basket.

FAST FACTS

The Basket Building weighs approximately 9,000 tons—the equivalent of 60 blue whales.

At 150 tons, the two handles alone weigh as much as one blue whale. They are heated in winter so they don't get iced up (which would make them even heavier).

There are 84 windows across all four sides of the building. The lights are left on at night so the whole structure lights up.

More than 4 million real Longaberger baskets would fit inside the building.

FAST FACTS

Judaism   Islam   Hinduism   Shintoism

Judaism is not the only religion to favor a particular color. For Muslims, the color green symbolizes nature and life, while for Hindus, saffron (an orange-yellow color) represents purity. Shinto temples in Japan are often painted red—a color associated with purification and protection from evil spirits.

The town's architecture mixes Spanish and North African styles.

These uneven wide steps and pretty floral displays are typically Moroccan.

Small town blues

Known as the **Blue Pearl**, Chefchaouen in Morocco is truly blue. All the buildings in its medina (old town) are **painted blue**, contrasting with the arid **Rif Mountains** surrounding the town. There is a religious meaning behind the **blue hue**.

First built as a 15th-century fortress, Chefchaouen turned blue in the 1930s, thanks to the local Jewish people. In Judaism, blue represents God, heaven, and sky. Ancient Jewish teachings state that dyeing thread with *tekhelel* (a natural indigo dye) would keep God in mind, a tradition that lives on in today's blue buildings.

The blue walls are thought to keep the town cool in summer and repel insects.

VENETIAN SPECTRUM

Burano is a multicolored island in Italy's Venetian lagoon. The houses are painted in glorious shades, with no two houses the same. The tradition originates with fishermen who painted their homes so they could spot them easily while fishing on the lagoon.

Peculiar plants

Why does the dragon's blood tree bleed and the Cannonball tree fire fruit? Take a stroll through Earth's boundless botanical garden and get to the roots of its secrets. Along the way, encounter the grandest growers, biggest bloomers, freakiest flowers, and stinkiest species.

As bark peels off at different times and in different places, the rainbow eucalyptus tree becomes a kaleidoscope of color. This fierce grower doubles in size each year until it reaches the dizzying height of 200 ft (60 m).

Fleeting flower

The supersized Titan arum is an **absolute showstopper** of the horticultural world. Taking many **years to flower**, botanists wait with baited breath for this unpredictable giant to bloom in **brief but breathtaking glory.**

This rare species grows in Sumatran rain forests, but its spectacular size has made it a favorite at botanical gardens. Its single flowerhead consists of a spadix (flower-bearing spike) surrounded by a leaf-like spathe. Flowering occurs only occasionally and lasts just days, accompanied by the rancid smell of rotting meat. When the flower dies, a single leaf the size of a small tree takes its place. This builds up food stores so the plant will eventually flower again.

The fleshy spadix heats up as the plant flowers and emits a powerful odor that attracts pollinating insects.

The protective spathe unfurls to reveal rings of flowers at the base of the spadix.

The **flowerhead emerging from the tuber adds 4 in (10 cm) to its height per day.**

POISON IN PARADISE

While Titan arum is smelly but harmless, *Daphne mezereum* is the opposite. Nicknamed the paradise plant, this species produces fragrant flowers, hiding the fact that it is deadly poisonous. Swallowing any part of this plant would lead to sudden sickness or even death.

The flower emerges from a huge tuber (underground stem) that can weigh more than 154 lb (70 kg).

FAST FACTS

The sizeable Titan arum flower is not a single flower—it is an inflorescence, or flower spike, bearing hundreds of flowers.

The century plant has a taller flower spike than the Titan arum, which it sends up every 20–30 years.

The talipot palm has the largest flower spike of all. Its flowers form an 26-ft (8-m) structure on top of the tree, which itself can be up to 82 ft (25 m) tall.

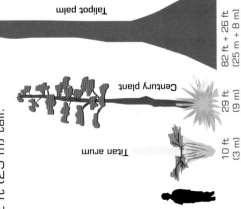

Titan arum — 10 ft (3 m)

Century plant — 29 ft (9 m)

Talipot palm — 82 ft + 26 ft (25 m + 8 m)

Hot lips

This plant may look like it is puckering up for a **big smooch**, but it's really saving all its love for **hummingbirds** and **butterflies**. The vibrant lip-like parts are actually **special leaves** designed to draw these feeders to its **sweet nectar**.

SNAPDRAGON SKULLS

Blooming in the sunshine, snapdragon flowers are colorful and beautiful, but things take a sinister turn when their seed pods dry out to resemble tiny skulls.

In this gap, the plant will grow its small white flowers. As butterflies and hummingbirds land on the flowers to drink nectar, they transfer pollen from flower to flower. This is essential for the plant's reproduction.

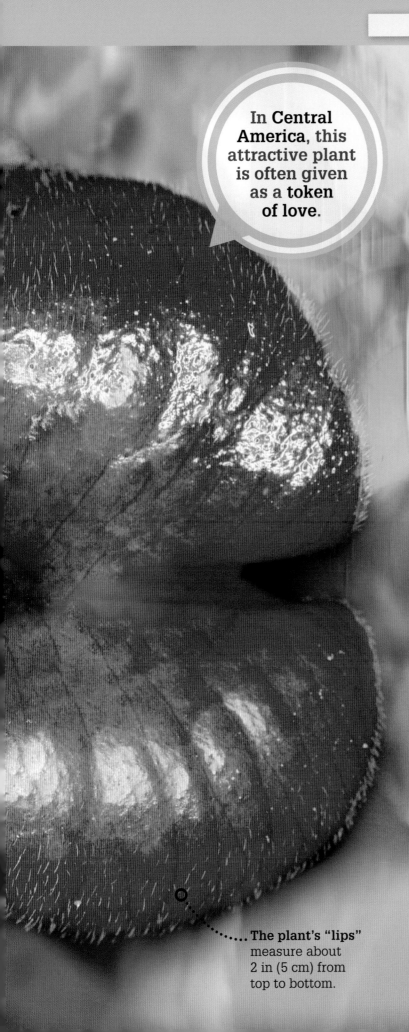

In **Central America**, this attractive plant is often given as a **token of love**.

······· **The plant's "lips"** measure about 2 in (5 cm) from top to bottom.

FAST FACTS

The hot lips plant is not the only plant to resemble something else. The bird of paradise plant looks just like its namesake, complete with colorful plumage, while the bleeding heart has bright pink, heart-shaped flowers. The yellow, orange, and red flowers of the flame lily resemble a roaring fire.

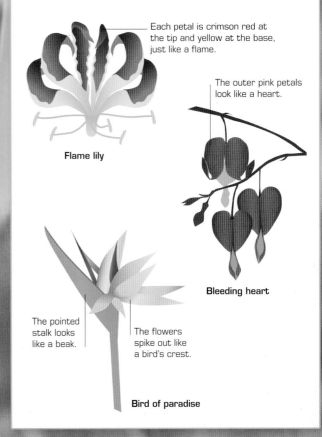

Each petal is crimson red at the tip and yellow at the base, just like a flame.

Flame lily

The outer pink petals look like a heart.

Bleeding heart

The pointed stalk looks like a beak.

The flowers spike out like a bird's crest.

Bird of paradise

Psychotria elata **is the scientific name** for the hot lips plant, which flowers in the humid forests of Costa Rica, Panama, and Colombia. Called bracts, the glossy red leaves are the perfect color to catch the eye of pollinators because butterfly and hummingbird eyes are very sensitive to red light.

Posturing petals

Some flowers can make you **look twice**.
Although their **real identities** are floral,
they resemble something **entirely different**.

Monkey business
The flowers of *Dracula simia*, or
the monkey orchid, are a dead ringer
for a mini monkey face. Preferring
high altitude habitats in Ecuador,
Colombia, and Peru, this unique
flower has also been grown in
captivity by orchid experts.

Budding baby
The *Anguloa uniflora* is a short orchid native to Peru and Chile, with each flower mimicking a baby swaddled in a blanket. The creamy, scented petals open in the summer months.

Buzzy bloomer
At first glance, this looks like bees drawing nectar from flowers. But look again. Growing around the Mediterranean and Middle East, this is the Woodcock Bee-orchid, a flower that closely resembles a bee.

Parrot petals
Native to Burma, Thailand, and India, the rare *Impatiens psittacina* is better known as the "parrot flower" because its pretty pastel petals look just like a parrot in flight.

Attack of the killer plants

There are at least 500 species of **carnivorous plant** on planet Earth, but nature's most famous meat-eater is the **Venus flytrap**. These jaws of death prey on **vulnerable insects**—and when they **snap shut**, there's no escape.

Unscrupulous collectors **dig up the wild plants**, putting the Venus flytrap at risk.

An unsuspecting **cricket** moves closer to the sweet nectar secreted from the Venus flytrap's open leaves.

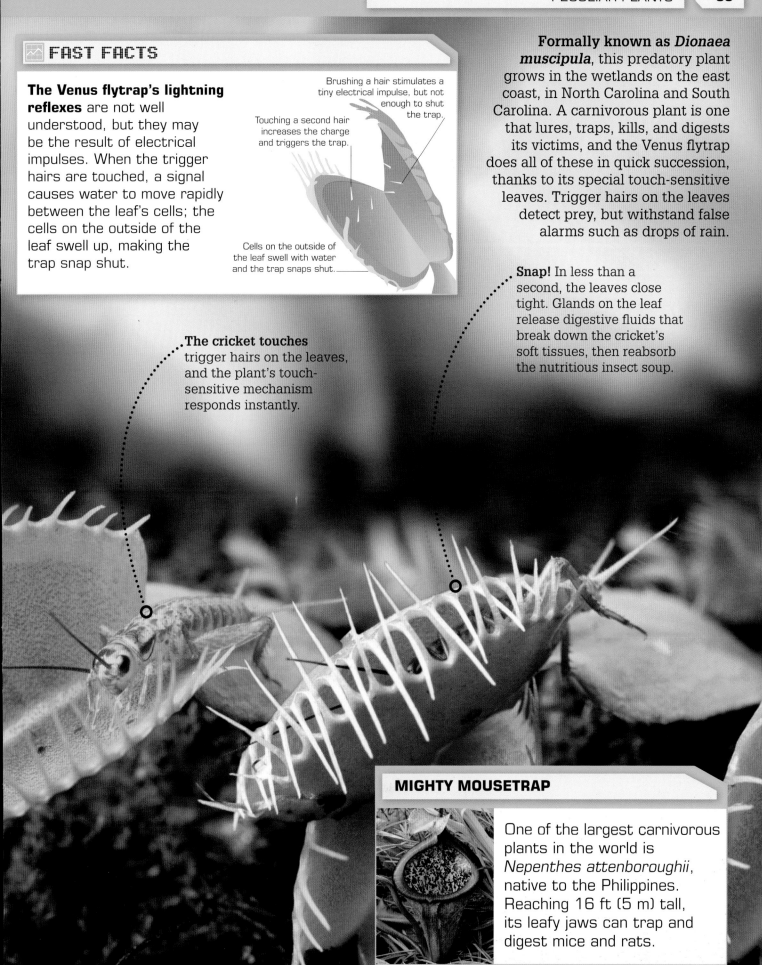

FAST FACTS

The Venus flytrap's lightning reflexes are not well understood, but they may be the result of electrical impulses. When the trigger hairs are touched, a signal causes water to move rapidly between the leaf's cells; the cells on the outside of the leaf swell up, making the trap snap shut.

Brushing a hair stimulates a tiny electrical impulse, but not enough to shut the trap.

Touching a second hair increases the charge and triggers the trap.

Cells on the outside of the leaf swell with water and the trap snaps shut.

Formally known as *Dionaea muscipula*, this predatory plant grows in the wetlands on the east coast, in North Carolina and South Carolina. A carnivorous plant is one that lures, traps, kills, and digests its victims, and the Venus flytrap does all of these in quick succession, thanks to its special touch-sensitive leaves. Trigger hairs on the leaves detect prey, but withstand false alarms such as drops of rain.

Snap! In less than a second, the leaves close tight. Glands on the leaf release digestive fluids that break down the cricket's soft tissues, then reabsorb the nutritious insect soup.

The cricket touches trigger hairs on the leaves, and the plant's touch-sensitive mechanism responds instantly.

MIGHTY MOUSETRAP

One of the largest carnivorous plants in the world is *Nepenthes attenboroughii*, native to the Philippines. Reaching 16 ft (5 m) tall, its leafy jaws can trap and digest mice and rats.

TREE ART

Tree shaping transforms plants into living art. Bending, weaving, and twisting help these sculptures take shape. The art form takes advantage of a process called inosculation—where tissue from two different plants, or parts of a plant that are touching, knits itself together.

Tree **bridges**

In the **forests of northeastern India**, rivers and streams are crossed using structures crafted from **ancient banyan trees**. Forged by tangled roots and vines, these living tree bridges are both a **natural wonder** and a master class in engineering.

The roots of the *Ficus elastica*, a type of banyan tree, twist into strong lattices.

Some of Cherrapunji's tree bridges are thought to be more than 500 years old.

Cherrapunji is one of the world's wettest places, so normal wooden structures would rot and break. Living bridges avoid this problem, enabling these children to get to school. By carefully guiding the strong, thick tree roots across rivers and voids, local Khasi people have grown permanent crossings that only get stronger over time. Patience and planning are required; they take 10 to 15 years to grow.

FAST FACTS

Some tree bridges are up to 100 ft (30 m) long, and can support the weight of 50 people or more at once. Local people use hollowed-out tree trunks to guide new roots into position and ensure the structure is strong.

Tree of blood

It can't fly and it doesn't breathe fire, but the **dragon's blood tree** can make one extraordinary claim to fame. The **bark of the tree bleeds**, leading to its use in magic and **medicine** since ancient times.

The dragon's blood tree (*dracaena cinnabari*) has an unusual appearance, with branches like white bony fingers reaching up to a crown of evergreen leaves. The blood-red sap is secreted naturally from cracks and cuts in the trunk. Harvesters open the existing fissures to collect the oozing sap, which has a variety of uses.

Legend claims the "blood" is an effective ingredient in love spells.

This slow-growing species is unique to the islands of Socotra in the Indian Ocean, off the coast of Yemen.

NEW BLOOD

The deep-red sap of the dragon's blood tree is an effective ingredient in dyes, varnish, adhesive, and incense. It has also been successful in treating cuts, bites, burns, and sores because the resin's healing properties reduce redness and swelling.

The dragon's blood tree grows up to 33 ft (10 m) in height.

FAST FACTS

Long, waxy leaves catch droplets of water from clouds of mist.

Water droplets run down the branches and trunk to the roots.

Although the dragon's blood tree looks like an umbrella, it is designed to collect, rather than repel, water. The long, waxy leaves gather moisture from the air and transport it down to the branches, trunk, and roots, enabling the tree to survive in Socotra's hot and dry climate.

Top trunks

Some trees are not just **part of the scenery**—they define the landscape with their **bizarre beauty**.

Tree of life
A prehistoric wonder in its native Africa, Australia, and Madagascar, the baobab is called "the tree of life." It can store huge amounts of water in its swollen trunk, enabling it to survive seasonal droughts.

Desert roots
The skinny and spiny Boojum tree soars above the other vegetation of the Sonoran Desert in California. Topping 50 ft (15 m), this species grows taller whenever there is rainfall, though it can survive for years without water.

Timber tunnel
Talk about a drive-through! This giant redwood named Chandelier Tree in Leggett, California, has a tunnel carved through its big base. Cars can pass through once a park entry fee has been paid.

Armed and deciduous

There's no better protected tree than the **Cannonball**. This **gargantuan grower** is found in South American forests and **attacks without warning**. Avoid being in the firing line when its weighty fruits **blast off**.

A member of the Brazil nut family, the Cannonball tree's proper name is *Couroupita guianensis*. Found in the rain forests of the Guianas (an area of northeastern South America) and in India, the tree's sweet-smelling flowers are used in perfumes and cosmetics. Its heavy fruits look like rusty cannonballs and when ripe, they fall to the ground and smash open with a bang. Locals use the fruit shells to craft containers and utensils.

TREE TREATMENT

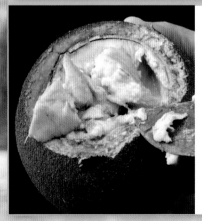

The Cannonball's bark, leaves, and fruit have been used in medicine for centuries. The beneficial bark is said to prevent colds and have antiseptic properties, while the leaves treat various skin diseases. The stinky fruit is used as a natural disinfectant for open wounds.

The tree towers up to 115 ft (35 m) and each fruit can weigh about 6 lb (3 kg).

The flesh of the large, round fruits is edible, but it gives off an overpowering stench.

FAST FACTS

Stamens bear fertile pollen.

Staminodes bear infertile pollen.

Infertile pollen attracts pollinators such as bees and bats.

Flowers of trees in the Brazil nut family have a unique structure. The fertile stamens form a fleshy ring, with a secondary mass of infertile stamens, called staminodes, making a kind of hood. Only the strongest pollinators—large bees or some bats—can lift the hood and collect the infertile pollen. As they do so, they brush the stamens, carrying the fertile pollen to the next flower they visit.

Algae attack!

China's **Yellow Sea** has recently gone green, caused by the nation's greatest **algae growth** to date. Since 2007, algae have swamped the waters every summer, but 2013's **big bloom** covered a record-breaking **11,158 sq miles** (28,900 sq km).

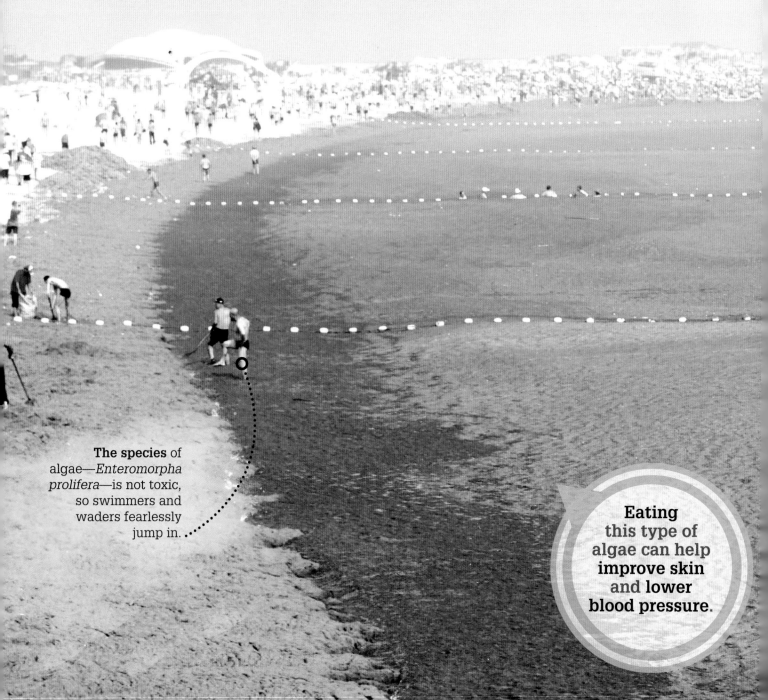

The species of algae—*Enteromorpha prolifera*—is not toxic, so swimmers and waders fearlessly jump in.

Eating this type of algae can help **improve skin** and **lower blood pressure.**

FAST FACTS

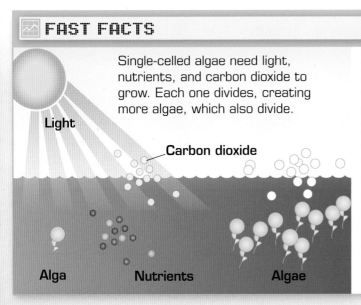

Single-celled algae need light, nutrients, and carbon dioxide to grow. Each one divides, creating more algae, which also divide.

Light

Carbon dioxide

Alga   Nutrients   Algae

Harmful algal blooms (HABs) form where colonies of sea-inhabiting plants, called algae, develop at a rapid rate, causing devastation to local marine life. In the right conditions, a population of algae can double in hours.

Despite the fun and frolic on the beach at Qingdao in the eastern Shandong province, this thick covering of algae stops sunlight and oxygen from penetrating the water, which suffocates sea life. Scientists don't know why the tide has turned green, but they agree the carpet of algae comes from an ecosystem imbalance, and is probably the result of human activity, such as agricultural and industrial pollution.

More than 8,200 tons of algae had to be removed from the beaches by city officials using bulldozers.

BRING ON THE BLUES

Electric blue algal blooms off the coast of Hong Kong look brilliantly bioluminescent, but what lies beneath is toxic pollution. Harmful *Noctiluca scintillans*, or sea sparkle, is flourishing because of excessive fertilizer and sewage. This devastates the landscape, killing local marine life.

Foul flower

Even the greenest fingers stop at the **corpse flower**. The biggest bloomer on Earth, this species is also the **stinkiest**, pervading the atmosphere with the **stench of rotten flesh**. What a relief that it's one of the world's **rarest flowers**!

ITSY-BITSY BLOOM

At the other end of the floral spectrum is the Asian watermeal plant, or *Wolffia globosa*. The size of a grain of rice, this green grower is the world's smallest flowering plant, and can be found floating in streams and ponds.

The corpse flower features in Indonesian tourist brochures as a symbol of the region's vibrant rain forests.

Each flower is made up of red lobes with white spots, resting on a cup-like structure.

FAST FACTS

The diameter of the largest *Rafflesia* flowers is equivalent to half the height of an adult man.

Though other flowers have larger clusters of flower heads, the corpse flower is the largest single flower. It can reach 3 ft (90 cm) wide and weigh 22 lb (10 kg).

The **flower buds** are used in **traditional medicine** to aid recovery after **childbirth.**

Rafflesia arnoldii, **as it is formally known**, uses disgusting odors to lure flies and other insects to pollinate the plant. Native to the rain forests of Borneo and Sumatra, it takes up to 10 months to bloom fully before the flower dies a week later. The plant has no leaves or stem, but lives as a parasite inside a host plant, hidden from view until the flower bud bursts through and the giant bloom unfurls.

Freaky flora

The most **incredible plants** can grow from a humble seed. Around the world some **dramatically different** forms have **taken root**.

Size matters
The giant water lily grows year-round in its native Brazil. With leaves more than 8 ft (2.5 m) long, it can carry up to 100 lb (45 kg) in weight, so these pigeons are no problem.

Tree tumbo
Considered by many to be an ugly and unruly plant, the tree tumbo plant just keeps on growing. It can survive for 1,500 years on the dew found in its isolated patch of the Namib Desert.

Monkey cup
The *Nepenthes* pitcher plant, which grows in Australia, Madagascar, and Southeast Asia, is known as the "monkey cup" because monkeys like the fluid inside its pitchers. Insects fall into this carnivorous vine's tropical trap in pursuit of nectar—but end up getting eaten themselves.

Hanging bangers
The *Kigelia africana*, or Sausage tree, can be seen across Africa's wetter regions. This whopper of a species reaches 66 ft (20 m) in height, with strange sausage-like fruits up to 35 in (90 cm) long.

Bicycle tree

Whoever got on this bike definitely **reached the end of the road**. No one knows how these wheels got **stuck in a tree**, and the **mystery** still drives locals totally bonkers years later.

The tree appears to have grown around the bike, but many argue the tree could not have lifted the bike from the ground because trees grow from the top, not the trunk.

TEMPLE TREES

The Buddhist temples of Angkor Wat in Cambodia are a stunning structural spectacle, but trees are the star attraction at one crumbling temple. Ta Prohm is a fusion of nature and architecture, where the great roots of silk cotton and strangler fig trees grow through the ruined roof.

FAST FACTS

The outer and inner bark protect the cambrium from animals, fungi, and the weather.

Outer bark

Inner bark

A layer under the bark called the cambrium has living cells that make the tree grow.

A tree can grow slowly around an object placed on, in, or close by it. The tree cannot move away, so it has to stop growing, grow away, or grow around the object when its trunk increases in size. It takes decades for an object to be truly stuck.

The bicycle was once red, but it has turned to rusty ruins while lodged in the trunk of this fir tree.

Local author **Berkeley Breathed** wrote a children's book about the **bicycle mystery**.

The riddle of the bicycle up a tree is legendary in Vashon Island, Washington. One story goes that a boy tied his bike to the tree before going to war in 1914, while town sheriff Don Puz is sure he left the bike behind in the 1950s. Sceptics insist it is nothing more than a hoax.

Out of **the blue**

The picture-perfect islands of the **Maldives** are famed for white beaches lapped by the Indian Ocean. But **Vaadhoo Island** is most breathtaking after dark when tiny plants turn the water electric blue. In this natural phenomenon, the **sparkling sea** appears to **reflect the starry night**.

Many sea creatures feed on **phytoplankton**, including **whales**, **sea snails**, and **jellyfish**.

Microscopic marine microbes called phytoplankton live in the sea. When they are disturbed by oxygen, a chemical reaction called bioluminescence (biological light) takes place—a flashing blue light is produced by the phytoplankton. This usually happens at sea when ships shake up oxygen underwater. Vaadhoo is unusual because bioluminescence occurs on the shore.

FAST FACTS

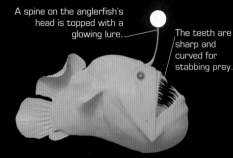

A spine on the anglerfish's head is topped with a glowing lure.

The teeth are sharp and curved for stabbing prey.

Many deep-sea creatures have evolved to produce their own bright light in the darkness. The anglerfish uses a bioluminescent "lantern" to tempt prey. Dangling from the fish's head, this houses bacteria that use chemicals produced by the fish to glow.

Each wave releases a flash of glowing blue in the many millions of phytoplankton washed up on the sand.

GLOW IN THE DARK

The Waitomo Caves in New Zealand are a haven for glowworms. This unique species—*Arachnocampa luminosa*—produces a striking light in the darkness. Boat trips into the caves take tourists to visit the glimmering glowworms.

Curious creatures

The animal kingdom is home to some truly fantastic fauna, slithering and sliding, racing and wriggling, and plunging and pouncing in every corner of nature's rich theater. Witness a breathtaking display of animal magic, with showstopping performances from dancing arachnids, acrobatic mammals, and reptile impersonators.

Poison dart frogs come in a spectrum of startling shades, sending a clear warning to predators to keep away. This brilliant blue species was only discovered in 1968, and is one of the world's only blue creatures.

Crab army

Every year up to **100 million red crabs** inhabiting Australia's **Christmas Island** migrate from their forest home to the Indian Ocean. This convoy of crustaceans travels 5 miles (9 km) with **only one goal**—reproduction.

Christmas Island red crabs can measure up to 4½ in (11.5 cm) across.

BAT CAVE

Another huge concentration of creatures can be found at Bracken Cave in Texas, home to the world's largest bat colony. About 20 million bats exit the cave each day at dusk searching for insects to feed on. It's one of nature's most amazing aerial sights.

Amorous male crabs will fight one another during the annual migration, competing for the attention of the females.

📈 FAST FACTS

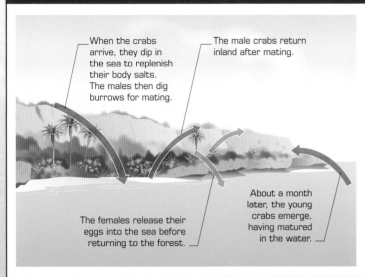

When the crabs arrive, they dip in the sea to replenish their body salts. The males then dig burrows for mating.

The male crabs return inland after mating.

The females release their eggs into the sea before returning to the forest.

About a month later, the young crabs emerge, having matured in the water.

The migration starts in early November and ends in January. Male crabs set off first, followed by the female crabs. It takes about a week for them to reach the shore. After mating, the males head back inland, followed soon after by the females.

The crabs are making their way to the sea. Mating takes place on the shore because the larval form of the crab has primitive gills that function only in water. Female crabs release eggs into the sea. The larvae hatch and grow in the water for about a month before congregating at the shore, ready to become mini air-breathing crabs. The tiny baby crabs then head back to the forest.

Male crabs reach the beach first and dig the burrows where mating will take place.

Jumbo **jitters**

It's every elephant's worst nightmare—just when you're chilling out by a watering hole, a **swarm of thousands of squawking birds** comes and spoils the serenity. **Overwhelmed by the frenzy**, this jumbo soon backed away.

Red-billed quelea are the world's most plentiful wild birds, with an adult breeding population of about 1.5 billion.

These tiny birds are red-billed quelea. They weigh just ½–¾ oz (15–20 g) each, but their huge number meant the total weight suddenly snapped a tree branch at Kenya's Satao Camp water hole in 2012. Taking to the skies, their deafening call and ferocious flapping of wings was too much for the big-eared elephant, who made a hasty retreat.

FAST FACTS

Flocks of red-billed quelea are a menace for farmers in Africa. One swarm can eat several fields of grain (56 tons) in a day—about the weight of seven elephants.

> The African elephant is the world's largest living land animal.

SCAREDY CATS

Despite being king of the beasts, lions have also been known to scare easily. A pack of lions was seen stalking an adult giraffe and baby in Kenya's Maasai Mara. Fearing for her offspring's safety, the giraffe charged and the pack ran away.

Dream teams

Teaming up works wonders in the animal kingdom. From aerial attacks to making mounds, there is definitely **strength in numbers**.

Golden jelly
Jellyfish Lake sits on a remote island of the Palau archipelago in the Pacific Ocean. This saltwater lake is the perfect home for millions of jellyfish because there are plenty of algae to feed on and no predators to avoid.

Spanish swarm
In 2004 the skies over the Spanish island of Fuerteventura were plagued by swarms of pink locusts from Africa. Their collective power wiped out one-third of the crops in some African countries, before 100 million of them flew on to Fuerteventura.

Wonder weavers
Named after their huge woven nests standing up to 13 ft (4 m) tall, sociable weaver birds of southern Africa work together to gather twigs, stems, and grass for their carefully constructed homes.

Massive mounds
There's no slacking in the termite team. Like ants and bees, this insect knows the power of many. Termite builders in Africa, Australia, and South America (above) create enormous mounds, with diameters stretching 98 ft (30 m). These homes can take five years to complete.

The journey south takes two months. The butterflies travel up to 100 miles (160 km) per day.

Marathon migration

It's a journey that would leave most of us exhausted: **Monarch butterflies cover 3,000 miles (4,800 km) on their annual flight from Canada to Mexico. The skies fill with millions of monarchs in the world's longest insect migration.**

The butterflies return to the same small area, and often the exact same trees, as previous generations.

Monarch butterflies can't survive the **cold Canadian winter** so they fly south to warmer climes. Most monarchs live for a maximum of eight weeks, but the generation that hatches at the end of the Canadian summer is different. Instead of mating and dying, they put all their energy into the migration, and can live for up to eight months. After spending the winter in Mexico, the migrating generation reproduce and their offspring make the journey back to Canada.

SUPPORTING THE SPECIES

Monarch butterflies only lay their eggs on milkweed plants, because they are the sole food of the newly hatched larvae. However, herbicide use has decreased the number of milkweed plants in North America. Conservationists are encouraging people to plant milkweeds at home, to create the habitat the monarchs need to survive.

In Mexico the monarch **butterflies** roost on the trunks and branches of fir trees to conserve energy.

⊞ FAST FACTS

Like all butterflies, monarchs go through four distinct stages in their life cycle. They are laid as eggs, which hatch into larvae, or caterpillars. The larva feeds, shedding its skin four or more times as its body gets bigger.

The larva then becomes a pupa, or chrysalis. Inside the pupa, the larva turns into an imago—an adult butterfly. The whole process from egg to butterfly is called metamorphosis.

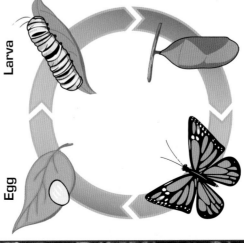

Egg

Larva

Pupa

Imago

World's wild webs

If **millions of spiders** congregate in one place, they can work as a team, spinning **enormous sheet webs** that **cover trees**, **hedges**, and **fields**. These wonder weavers transform the landscape with their **intricate designs**.

FAST FACTS

The spider with the longest legs is a species discovered in a cave in Laos in 2001—the giant huntsman spider. It measures 12 in (30 cm) from the tip of one leg to the tip of its opposite leg. The biggest spider by weight is the Goliath bird-eater, a species of South American tarantula that weighs in at 2½ oz (70 g).

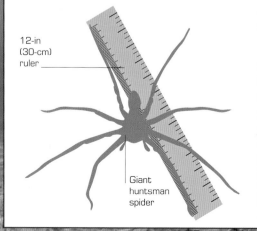

12-in (30-cm) ruler

Giant huntsman spider

These webs are so dense that trees appear to be covered in nets.

When water levels rose several yards above Sindh's normal levels, wildlife headed for the trees to survive.

Spiders made these webs when a decade's worth of rain dropped on Sindh in a week.

In 2010 many trees were blanketed by giant webs in Sindh, Pakistan, when heavy monsoon rains flooded large areas. Spiders and other web-spinning creatures living on the ground had to seek shelter. They climbed trees to escape the flood waters, and their handiwork was visible for all to see.

ANIMAL ORACLES

Some creatures can predict natural disasters. Birds take flight when they sense a storm coming, and researchers in Florida found sharks swim into deeper water before a hurricane.

Strutting spider

Australia's **peacock spider** makes all the right **moves** in a bid to impress the ladies. Getting into the groove is easy with **eight legs** and a multicolored stomach flap to shake.

Peacock spiders have six eyes and can see fine details in color from yards away.

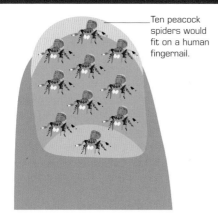

Ten peacock spiders would fit on a human fingernail.

Peacock spiders are tiny—adults grow to only about ¹⁄₁₀ in (4 mm) long. Despite this, these aptly named jumping spiders are capable of pouncing more than 20 times their body length.

The colorful stomach flap of the male spider is lifted like a fan during the courtship dance. At other times it remains folded away out of sight.

The courtship dance of the male peacock spider involves a series of attention-grabbing jumps, sways, and struts to attract partners. His colors and moves are studied by the female before she decides if he is a suitable mate. If she isn't interested, she may attack and eat her suitor instead!

After mating, the **peacock spider** will get up and moving again to **find more females.**

This spider gets its name from the equally flashy peacock bird.

PLUMAGE OF PARADISE

The mating efforts of the bird of paradise are hard to ignore. The male is transformed by showcasing his big, brilliant blue frontage before he performs an impressive courtship dance. His performance must be perfect to win over the drably colored female.

Bloated
bloodsuckers

Ticks are the **vampires** of the bug brigade, gorging on blood for survival. The **Rocky Mountain wood tick** swells to many times its original size after a grand feast. **Bloated on blood**, the sucker drops off its weakened host.

At home in the higher ground of Colorado, the Rocky Mountain wood tick (*Dermacentor andersoni*) is a three-host species. It feeds three times in its three-year lifetime—as a newly hatched larva, as a nymph, and as an adult. While small creatures suffice for its first two feeds, this tick's last supper features deer, sheep, or even people!

An adult wood tick can **live for up to 600 days** without feeding.

FAST FACTS

Eggs

Larva

Adult

Nymph

Rocky Mountain wood ticks are best avoided. At all stages in their life cycle, they can transmit tick-borne diseases to humans, cats, and dogs. In most cases, the victim has just 24 hours to remove the tick from the skin (by grasping it with blunt tweezers) before the body is infected.

The adult wood tick is armed and dangerous, with a hard shell and a ruthless bite. ......

Before

The tick feeds on its host and grows until it is fully engorged with blood.

Ticks are arachnids—closely related to spiders. There are up to 900 species of tick.

After

MIGHTY MICROBUG

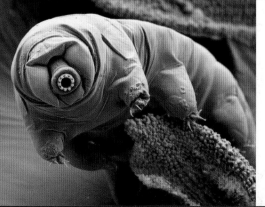

The tardigrade is only 0.04 in (1 mm) long, but virtually indestructible. Dropped in boiling water or left in frozen ice, this little fighter won't flinch. Remove its water supply for a decade or launch it into space, and there's still no harm done.

Pouncing parasites

Parasites need **no invitation**. These organisms find a **host organism**, attach themselves to it, and **reap all the benefits**.

Tongue-tied
Inside the mouth of this pink anemonefish is a tongue-eating louse parasite. *Cymothoa exigua* enters through the fish's gills, latches onto its tongue, and settles in for a feast. When the tongue is all eaten up, the louse itself serves as a replacement.

The frog and the flatworm
Parasitic flatworms give tadpoles a terrible time, forcing themselves into the tissue that will later become frog's legs. The adult frog ends up with deformed, missing, or extra limbs.

Shell shock
The *Leucochloridium paradoxum* flatworm infests the digestive systems of birds and passes to snails feeding on bird droppings. The parasite moves to the snail's tentacles where it is mistaken for caterpillars by hungry birds, and the cycle continues.

Hatching a plan
The female sabre wasp lays its eggs on the larvae of the wood wasp using its large ovipositor to drill into infested wood. When the eggs hatch into larvae they eat their hosts alive.

Parasite for sore eyes

Blink and you'll miss them, but **minuscule parasites** have taken up residence on your **eyelashes**. Here, they've found a comfortable home and an **endless food supply** without even an invite. And the older you get, the more mites come to stay!

Each **eyelash mite** is just **0.01 in (0.3 mm) long**—difficult to see with the naked eye.

Though eyelashes are the preferred location, these mites will also infest the nose, cheeks, and forehead.

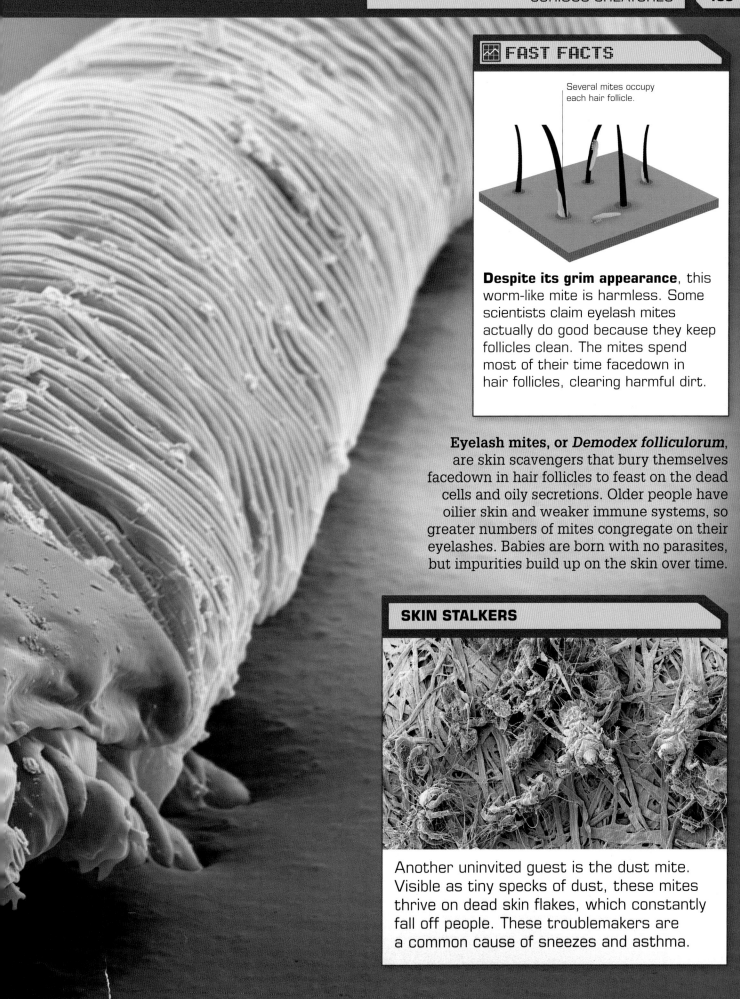

Several mites occupy each hair follicle.

Despite its grim appearance, this worm-like mite is harmless. Some scientists claim eyelash mites actually do good because they keep follicles clean. The mites spend most of their time facedown in hair follicles, clearing harmful dirt.

Eyelash mites, or *Demodex folliculorum*, are skin scavengers that bury themselves facedown in hair follicles to feast on the dead cells and oily secretions. Older people have oilier skin and weaker immune systems, so greater numbers of mites congregate on their eyelashes. Babies are born with no parasites, but impurities build up on the skin over time.

SKIN STALKERS

Another uninvited guest is the dust mite. Visible as tiny specks of dust, these mites thrive on dead skin flakes, which constantly fall off people. These troublemakers are a common cause of sneezes and asthma.

This caterpillar is the **larval stage** of the *Hemeroplanes triptolemus* moth.

Snake in the grass

When is a snake not a snake? When it's a **caterpillar**! This extraordinary disguise is **self-defense**. The snake mimic hawkmoth caterpillar does an **uncanny impression** of a scary snake to avoid its forest predators.

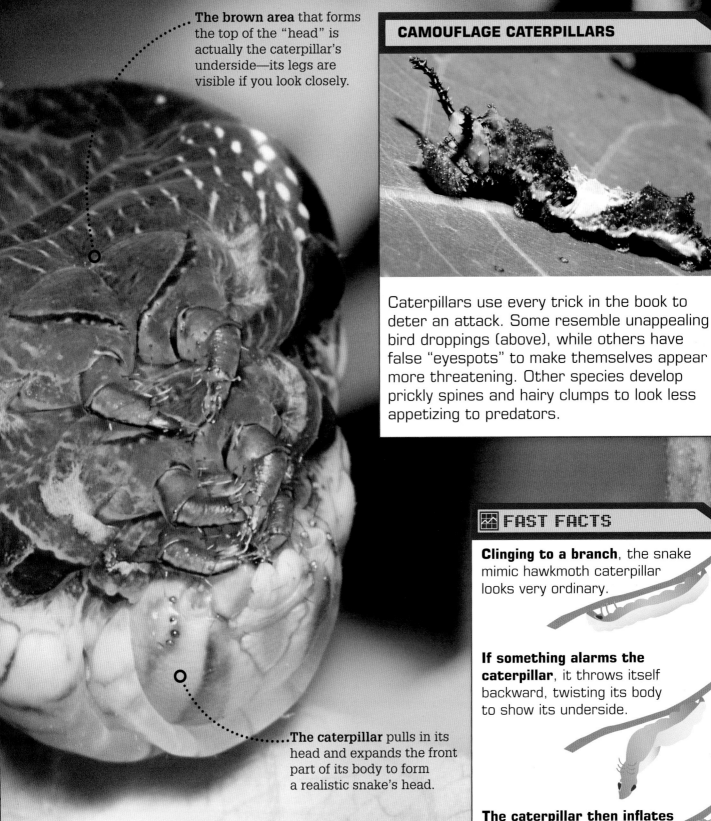

The brown area that forms the top of the "head" is actually the caterpillar's underside—its legs are visible if you look closely.

CAMOUFLAGE CATERPILLARS

Caterpillars use every trick in the book to deter an attack. Some resemble unappealing bird droppings (above), while others have false "eyespots" to make themselves appear more threatening. Other species develop prickly spines and hairy clumps to look less appetizing to predators.

The caterpillar pulls in its head and expands the front part of its body to form a realistic snake's head.

If this hawkmoth caterpillar feels threatened, it immediately takes on snake-like characteristics and behavior. Pulling in its legs and head, the caterpillar adopts a slithering motion. Its underside grows larger, giving the semblance of a snake's head. The body is large by caterpillar standards and covered in scales, ensuring this species is one convincing masquerader.

FAST FACTS

Clinging to a branch, the snake mimic hawkmoth caterpillar looks very ordinary.

If something alarms the caterpillar, it throws itself backward, twisting its body to show its underside.

The caterpillar then inflates the head-end of its body to create a realistic-looking snake's head.

Flying figures

Considered a **sign of good fortune** in its native Central and South America, the **Callicore butterfly's** lucky numbers are **88** and **89**. Emblazoned across each wing, the **striking digits** help this species to **attract mates** amid the flora and fauna.

These high-speed fliers travel solo through their tropical rain forest homes.

WINDOW WINGS

You can see right through the Glasswing butterfly. Its transparent wings resemble panes of glass, helping the species evade predators in its Central American domain.

The **88'89 butterfly** lands on people in summer to dine on their sweat.

FAST FACTS

Tiny scales scatter the light, creating beautiful iridescent colors.

Butterfly wings are covered with thousands of tiny scales made from a substance called chitin. These dusty scales give the insects their striking colors, as well as helping to regulate their body temperature.

The numerals 89 or 88 appear clearly on the underside of each wing.

The exact markings of the 88'89 butterfly depend on the specific subspecies. There are 12 types, with the markings taking a different form, color, and shape each time. Sadly, the number of Callicores is dwindling—they are often killed for their exotic wings, which are used in the production of tourist souvenirs.

Devil in **disguise**

Is it a leaf? Is it tree bark? No, it's the **Satanic leaf-tailed gecko**. Cleverly disguised as a rotting leaf, Madagascar's **camouflage king** has red eyes, pointy horns, and a taste for night hunting. It's nature's most **devilish deceiver**.

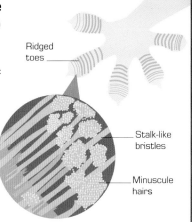

 **FAST FACTS**

Geckos have sticky toe pads that allow them to cling to polished walls. Each toe is ridged and covered in thousands of tiny bristles, which are divided into billions of microscopic hairs. These hairs lock with irregularities in the surface the gecko is climbing, giving it grip.

Ridged toes

Stalk-like bristles

Minuscule hairs

Leaf-tailed geckos have **no eyelids. They** use their long tongues to wipe away dust.

This mini-monster epitomizes survival of the fittest, having adapted gradually to become today's extraordinary leaf impersonator. Snakes and rats target the gecko—if the disguise fails, the brave battler falls to the forest floor, hoping to disappear in the foliage, or leaps to a higher branch for shelter.

MOSSY MASK

Madagascar's mossy leaf-tailed gecko is another master of disguise. Its color and markings make it look exactly like mossy tree bark. A fringe of skin flattens the gecko against the tree so that, when still, it blends seamlessly into its forest habitat.

The twisted body and veiny skin echo the detail of a dry leaf, which ensures the gecko blends in with its forest home.

The mottled tail appears to have sections missing, as though it has withered over time.

In hiding

Standing out from the crowd leaves you **vulnerable** in the **animal kingdom**. Where conflicts are fierce, food is scarce, and lives are on the line, **blending in** can be the best bet for **survival**.

Sly fox

As snowy white as its tundra home, the Arctic fox blends in easily with the icy winter surroundings. But this colored coat changes with the seasons. Summer sees the fox sport a reddish brown fur better suited to the bare rock and plants.

Tree mimic

The African scops owl uses its camouflaged plumage and twig-like ear tufts to conceal itself, then swoops suddenly on insects and rodents.

Secretive spider
Europe's green huntsman spider is the perfect shade to merge with nearby foliage. The arachnid can move virtually unseen by both predators and prey.

Armed attacker
This vivid inhabitant of Australia's Great Barrier Reef resembles part of the coral, but is actually a stonefish. With toxic spines ready, it waits to ambush passing prey.

Adaptable amphibian
The African red toad spends its days hiding under logs or on dead leaves, using its colors and patterned skin to keep safe, while nights are spent searching out insects.

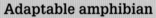

Goat gymnasts

No kidding—the **goats of Tamri village** in Morocco show great agility when **searching for their favorite food**. These nimble nibblers claw, jump, and scramble up **argan trees** to reach their beloved berries, setting in motion a **practice** that's been around for centuries.

INTREPID IBEX

In 2010 a herd of Alpine ibex walked across the nearly vertical face of Italy's Cingino Dam. Despite the 164-ft (50-m) drop beneath them, the agile ibex searched for a snack—salt and lichen between the dam's stones.

Argan berries are a good source of income in this otherwise barren land. Goats gorge on them and pass the hard nuts in their droppings. Locals collect the droppings then remove and wash the nuts. These are ground and pressed to make expensive argan oil, used in salad dressings and cosmetic treatments.

The olive-like argan berry is perfect nourishment in an area where food is scarce.

The **Tamri goats** can climb 30 ft (9 m) up to the **treetops**.

Goats are curious by nature, revelling in opportunities to climb and explore.

📊 **FAST FACTS**

Goats are good climbers because of their cloven hoofs. The two sides push apart to grip a surface. The hoof has a soft inner part that aids grip, while the animal's dewclaws help provide stability.

Dewclaws

Hard outer hoof

Hoof is cloven (split into two)

Soft inner part

Dance fever

The lord of the dance on the island of Madagascar is the **Verreaux's sifaka**. Fancy footwork has made this **species of lemur** a global sensation, but these moves have real purpose. **Whirling and twirling** through the forest helps them **evade predators**.

Sifakas have splayed feet, which make it difficult to walk. Instead, they "dance" by hopping sideways rapidly on their back legs.

PIG PARADISE

Pigs can't fly, but they can swim! A family of wild porkers enjoys an idyllic island lifestyle on Big Major Cay in the Bahamas. They take daily dips, heading for boats in case people drop food. Sailors are said to have left the pigs on the island, intending to return for a bacon bonanza, but they never did.

As dawn breaks, groups of Verreaux's sifakas perform a dazzling dance display. They swing, leap, and bound their way to the feeding grounds where they forage for food. Only in the safety of the treetops can they sit back to munch on a variety of plants unique to the African island.

The sifaka holds its arms up near its head for balance, while its springy step means it can escape fast, should a predator attack.

Verreaux's sifakas are named after their distinctive noisy cry that sounds like "shif-auk!"

📈 FAST FACTS

Sifakas are not only nimble on the ground. They also use their powerful hind legs and upright position to leap from tree to tree, often clearing distances of more than 30 ft (9 m).

In-flight fight

At first glance, **fur and feathers** appear to have forged an **incredible friendship** in this photograph. The weasel **hitches a ride** on the woodpecker's back as they soar the skies together. In reality, this picture catches on camera the **ultimate airborne animal attack**.

A **sign** now marks the spot where the sensational **snap** was taken.

ANIMAL ALLIANCES

The animal kingdom can be about forming friendships rather than fighting foes. In Ireland a dog named Ben and a dolphin named Duggie enjoy friendly swims together, while best pals Fum the cat and Gebra the owl were viewed playing together by one million people on YouTube.

In 2015 amateur photographer Martin Le-May shot this image in Hornchurch Country Park, London, UK, but the picture doesn't tell the full story. The weasel attacked the woodpecker and refused to give up, even when the bird took flight. An aerial scrap ensued before the weasel tumbled and the woodpecker escaped.

FAST FACTS

The least weasel's body is just bigger than an adult hand.

The tail can be up to 3⅛ in (8 cm) long.

The least weasel is the world's smallest carnivore. Measuring only 4⅓–10⅕ in (11–26 cm) and weighing as little as 9/10 oz (25 g), it has been known to kill prey up to 10 times its weight. It is found throughout Europe, North America, and parts of Asia.

The carnivorous least weasel typically attacks large prey, such as rabbits, mice, frogs, and birds.

The European green woodpecker often leaves itself vulnerable to attack because it forages on the ground for ants.

Dedicated dad

Assumptions about the **female of the species** giving birth are true of most creatures, but **reproduction** is **different** for seahorses. It's **the male** of this odd-looking fish species that **experiences pregnancy and childbirth**, to sighs of relief from female seahorses everywhere!

The young seahorses, or fry, emerge from the opening in the brood pouch.

Muscular contractions expel the young seahorses from the pouch.

SHARK SPAWN

The frilled shark has the longest gestation period of any species. Like seahorses, they are ovoviviparous—their young hatch from eggs inside the parent's body. Embryos then grow inside the mother for a staggering three and a half years before finally being born.

This male seahorse's pouch is full of fry. Smaller species may carry 50 offspring, while bigger types nurture up to 2,000.

The female seahorse makes the eggs inside her body. Male and female entwine tails and perform a long courtship dance that ends with the female depositing the eggs in the male's pouch. The male fertilizes the eggs and they hatch inside his pouch. The embryos take in everything they need, from oxygen to food, in a gestation period that lasts up to four weeks.

Fewer than five in 1,000 young seahorses survive into adulthood.

📈 **FAST FACTS**

Horse-like head

Long snout

Brood pouch

Grasping tail

Male

Female

Seahorses are marine fish found in warm, shallow waters all over the world. Their bodies are protected by bony plates, rather than scales. Poor swimmers, they use their grasping tail to cling to vegetation and their long snout to suck up plankton.

Shoal-stopper

Millions of sardines cause an **amazing annual spectacle** by swimming in one **supersized shoal** along South Africa's eastern coastline, to the delight of hungry ocean predators. The **"Sardine Run"** is plagued with danger, and the reason for this **mega migration** is unknown.

MARINE MIGRATION

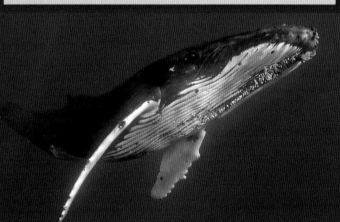

From small sardines to whopper whales, all kinds of marine life migrate. Humpback whales break the record for the longest mammal migration, covering 5,160 miles (8,300 km) from Pacific waters off Costa Rica all the way to Antarctica.

A baitball is 33–65 ft (10–20 m) in diameter and usually lasts only 10–20 minutes.

Under threat, the sardines squash up into a neat baitball, so that no individual fish can be singled out.

FAST FACTS

The migrating sardines travel north along the east coast of South Africa, from their spawning ground of Agulhas Bank to the subtropical waters off the coast of Durban. The huge shoals can be 9⅓ miles (15 km) long.

South Africa

Durban

Cape Town

Agulhas Bank

Sardine run

Sardines are an integral part of the ocean food chain, with their sheer quantity sustaining many other fish species.

As the tiny fish make their journey, predators gather for a feeding frenzy. Dolphins round up the sardines into baitballs, while birds descend from the skies and sharks converge in the water. The risky migration's motive is unclear, but it may be that the southern waters become too cold for the sardines.

Murky monsters

A **monster's ball** is underway in the deep ocean. You'll want to keep your head above water once you see these **bizarre beasts** of the **seabed**.

Confident cucumber
The transparent sea cucumber shows everything off, including its digestive system! Formally known as *Enypniastes*, it feeds on sediment and moves around on its tentacles.

Jaw-dropper

The scaleless black dragonfish is a scary sight. With oversized jaws and razor-sharp teeth, this predatory fish produces a light to lure smaller fish and crustaceans to their deaths.

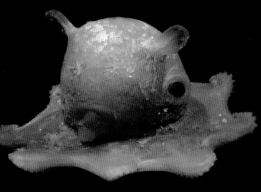

Squashed octopus

Despite its name, the flapjack octopus is not remotely appetizing! The name comes from its compressed bottom, which makes this species appear flatter than other octopuses.

Fearsome fangs

Nicknamed "ogrefish" for its off-putting appearance, *Anoplogaster cornuta* has a tough, bony body. Commonly known as the fangtooth, it is the fish with the biggest teeth in relation to its body size.

Forces of nature

When nature is unleashed in all its glory, the results are spectacular. Super storms tear the skies apart, vast dust clouds leave chaos in their wake, and fiery tornadoes cause carnage on the ground. Nature's mysteries also remind us of its all-pervading power— from stones that seem to sail across the desert to strange sand structures sculpted by lightning.

A fire rainbow, or circumhorizontal arc, forms in high-altitude wispy summer clouds where plate-shaped ice crystals are present. The sun's rays must penetrate the ice crystals at an exact angle for this phenomenon to occur.

When ice attacks

Forget the **thunderous roars** of a violent storm—a less dramatic storm produces the most **spectacular** scenes. **Ice storms** happen when **supercooled rain** freezes as it hits the ground, transforming the landscape into a **frozen fairy-tale world**.

This storm only lasted **five minutes**, but it was enough to turn **cars and trees** into **ice statues**.

STORM DAMAGE

The crust of frozen rain that coats everything after an ice storm can be so thick and heavy that it makes structures like these electricity pylons collapse.

FAST FACTS

Warm air

Cold air

Rain
When frozen precipitation passes through warm air, it melts and falls to the ground as rain.

Freezing rain
If frozen precipitation melts in warm air, but cools rapidly as it nears the ground, it freezes on contact.

Sleet
If frozen precipitation thaws in shallow warm air, it re-freezes as sleet before it hits the ground.

Snow
When frozen precipitation falls through cold air, it reaches the surface as snow.

Icicles dangling from these tree branches follow the direction of the wind blowing in from Lake Geneva.

Roads and pavement become a treacherous ice rink.

Ice storms are rare events that occur when rain warm air and meets cold air near the ground. The rain freezes on impact, covering everything in a thick, frosty coating. Switzerland's Lake Geneva experienced this ice storm in 2012.

Sailing stones

Death Valley is the USA's hottest spot. This remote desert landscape provides **a perfect backdrop** for science-fiction blockbusters such as *Star Wars*, but something stranger than fiction happens here. Heavy rocks **inexplicably move around.** From magnetic fields to alien activity, theories abounded. Finally, we learned the truth.

Since 1948 scientific research has left no stone unturned. The breakthrough came in 2014, when stones were seen moving on camera. Floating ice proved to be the mischief-maker. On cold nights, thin sheets of ice develop, which then melt down into smaller pieces in the daytime sunshine. Wind pushes the ice along, carrying the rocks with it and depositing them elsewhere.

Each rock travels 6–20 ft (2–6 m) per minute, but in the desert this motion is hard to notice with the naked eye.

STONE COMMANDMENTS

These granite slabs in Elbert County, Georgia, are a mystery set in stone. Known as the Georgia Guidestones, they appeared in 1979 engraved with 10 guidelines for people to follow, which include avoiding useless officials and leaving room for nature. No one knows who wrote the list or who placed the stones.

Despite its name, Death Valley is home to more than **400 species** of animal.

Early theories suggested that strong winds were responsible for moving the stones. But hurricane-force gusts would be needed to overcome the weight of the heavy rocks.

Racetrack Playa is a dry lake in Death Valley, dotted with large rocks that have fallen onto the plain from the surrounding mountains.

The moving stones can weigh more than 660 lb (300 kg), with some making tight turns and switching direction.

FAST FACTS

A floating sheet of ice is pushed along by wind.

Caught in the ice, the rock moves forward.

Wind

Shallow water

The weight of the stone leaves a trail behind.

Rainfall creates a shallow pool in the playa, which then freezes over as the temperature drops. A swift rise in temperature breaks up the ice into smaller, floating sheets. Wind then pushes the ice sheets over the pond. Any rocks caught in the ice sheet are easily carried along by the buoyant ice, inscribing a trail in the mud as they go.

Whipping up a dust storm

The incredible **power of nature** is seen when a violent dust storm blows up, filling the skies with inescapable banks of **suffocating cloud**. Tons of whirling sand or soil are swept along by high winds, leaving a **trail of devastation** behind.

FAST FACTS

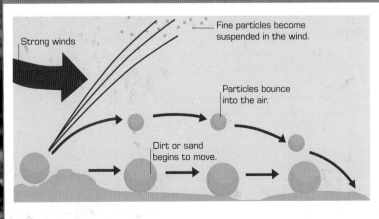

Fine particles become suspended in the wind.

Strong winds

Particles bounce into the air.

Dirt or sand begins to move.

Strong winds whip up particles of dust or sand. The pieces move along the ground, then begin to jump into the air. As they break up into smaller pieces, they are carried off by the wind.

Dust storms are most likely to occur during droughts, when sand or soil is loose and dry. Carried on the wind, billowing dust clouds can envelop entire cities, choking the inhabitants and damaging buildings. This huge dust cloud engulfed the desert city of Riyadh, Saudi Arabia, in March 2009. After the storm passed, parts of the city were left beneath several tons of sand.

DUST DEVILS

Resembling mini tornadoes, dust devils are small-scale whirlwinds, spinning dust in a vertical column of air over the ground. They are less dangerous than their name suggests, usually lasting only a few minutes and rarely causing any damage.

This massive storm on March 10, 2009, reduced **visibility** in Riyadh to **zero**.

Flights were grounded at Riyadh's airport as the control tower and runways were blanketed in thick dust.

When lightning strikes

No matter how long you keep staring and guessing, these **oddball objects** are almost impossible to fathom. Called **fulgurites**, they are the **remarkable and rare** result of what can happen when lightning strikes planet Earth.

ETERNAL STORM

There is never any calm before the storm at Venezuela's Catatumbo River. Thanks to a unique bank of storm clouds, an "everlasting storm" rages here, producing 1.2 million lightning strikes a year. Known as Catatumbo lightning, this incredible light show is visible 250 miles (400 km) away.

A fulgurite is formed when a lightning bolt with a minimum temperature of 3,270°F (1,800°C) strikes sand or rock. Heat melts the substance on impact, fusing the grains into natural glass tubes that follow the branching structure of the lightning bolt deep underground. Over time, the sand around the fulgurite shifts, exposing the fragile tube. Most fulgurites are made from sand, reflected in the unusually high number in the Sahara Desert.

With its branch-like formation, this sand fulgurite has a rough exterior covered in sand particles, but its interior is smooth and resembles glass.

Fulgurite comes from the Latin word for "thunderbolt."

Sand cools and solidifies quickly after the lightning strike to create the fulgurite. Its size depends on the power of the strike and the depth of the sand.

FAST FACTS

The longest fulgurite on record

was dug up by researchers from the University of Florida in 1996. This impressive tube had two branches, the longest of which was about 16 ft (5 m) long.

Fulgurites are very fragile, so great care must be taken when digging them up.

The fulgurite is formed underground.

The forked shape of the fulgurite shows the lightning's path.

Super storms

Most thunderstorms develop from **updraughts of rising air**, with the most violent and speedy ones called **supercells**. These long-lasting storms are rare but deadly—they can **unleash havoc** in the form of whirling tornadoes, giant hailstones, punishing winds, and flash floods. Take cover!

Earth experiences about 45,000 thunderstorms a day, but only a few of these are supercells, the worst of all storms. Created by rapidly rotating updrafts of warm, moist air, these super storms carry huge amounts of water and bring extreme weather. The top of the thunderclouds can reach as high as 10 miles (16 km) into the air, while the base may be only 1,640 ft (500 m) above the ground.

Foreboding dark cumulonimbus clouds congregate in the skies before a supercell storm.

A supercell storm can last for two to six hours, often leaving behind considerable damage.

FAST FACTS

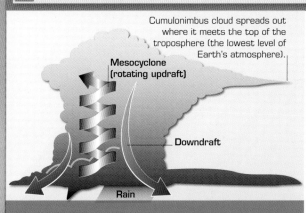

Cumulonimbus cloud spreads out where it meets the top of the troposphere (the lowest level of Earth's atmosphere).

Mesocyclone (rotating updraft)

Downdraft

Rain

Thunderstorms are formed by warm updrafts rising to create cumulonimbus clouds. Cold rain drags air down, creating a cold downdraft. When there is more downdraft than updraft, the storm fizzles out. In a supercell the updrafts and downdrafts are in balance, so the storm can keep going for hours. The mesocyclone (rapidly rotating updraft) at the storm's core carries huge amounts of water upward so the cloud grows bigger and bigger.

Lightning is about 54,000°F (30,000°C)— hotter than the surface of the sun.

BALL LIGHTNING

During a supercell storm, other odd things can happen. Luminous, ball-shaped objects have appeared a few yards above the ground, bouncing around in a random pattern. Scientists can't agree on the reason for this phenomenon, known as ball lightning.

Weird weather

Extreme weather can be **challenging** for meteorologists to predict, and the consequences are often **devastating**.

Twisting tornado
More than 1,200 tornadoes rip across the USA every year, traveling up to 200 mph (320 kph) and leaving trails of devastation behind them. Canada has the second highest number—this one is twisting across Elie, Manitoba.

Killer Katrina
When Hurricane Katrina tore across Florida in 2005, it became the USA's costliest natural disaster. Winds topped 175 mph (280 kph) and nearly 2,000 people died.

Wild waves
Triggered by a huge offshore earthquake, the Indian Ocean tsunami on December 26, 2004, occurred without warning and heaped havoc on southern Asia. Giant waves devastated coastal communities and killed more than 200,000 people, displacing thousands more.

Heavy hail
In 2003 a thunderstorm in Moses, New Mexico, produced hailstones the size of golf balls. Huge hail can easily smash car windshields and injure people on the ground.

Deadly shower
All sorts of things have fallen from the skies, including frogs, bats, fish, insects, jellyfish, and worms. Strong winds can take creatures from shallow ponds and carry them until they fall back down to Earth. In 2011 about 1,000 dead birds mysteriously rained over Arkansas.

Lava and lightning

One of nature's most **explosive** combinations occurs when an **erupting volcano** generates an **electrical storm**. The reason for this **lightning bolt** out of the blue is still not fully understood.

EXPLODING PIZZA

The most explosive place in the solar system is Io, one of Jupiter's moons. The crater-faced surface earned Io the nickname "pizza moon." Io has hundreds of active volcanoes, and volcanic plumes can rise up to 186 miles (300 km) above its surface.

At least **150 episodes** of **volcanic lightning** have been documented over the last **200 years**.

Lightning is caused by a build up of static electric charges. Scientists are not sure what creates the charge during a volcanic eruption, but they think that hot ash particles in the volcanic cloud may rub together, producing a charge of static that triggers sparks of lightning. This is similar to what happens inside storm clouds, where ice particles collide and create a charge.

Volcanic lightning illuminates a cloud of ash and lava spewing from Japan's Sakurajima volcano in January 2013.

FAST FACTS

Positive charge

Negative charge

Lightning occurs when the attraction between positive and negative charges is big enough.

The negative charge at the base of the cloud causes a positive charge on the ground.

When ice particles in a storm cloud rub together, they gain electrons (becoming negatively charged) or lose electrons (becoming positively charged). The positively charged particles accumulate at the top of the cloud, while the negatively charged ones settle at the bottom. When the difference in charge becomes great enough, the energy is discharged as lightning.

UFO clouds

Hovering like a **flying saucer** in the sky, these amazing **layered** cloud formations are called **lenticular** (lentil-shaped) **clouds**. They form near **mountain ranges**, where mountains disturb the airflow and create **pressure waves**.

As air flows through and exits the rear of the cloud, the cloud droplets in the air evaporate, becoming water vapor. Because water vapor is an invisible part of the air, the cloud vanishes here.

CLOUD COVER

One of the world's cloudiest places is South Africa's Prince Edward Islands, with about 800 hours of sunshine all year. Sun lovers should go to Yuma in Arizona, which has more than 4,000 hours of sunshine annually.

The cloud's layers reveal the different layers of air flow in the atmosphere. Each layer of air forms a layer of the cloud.

Stacked like **pancakes**, each **lentil-shaped** layer of cloud forms on top of layers of air.

Locals in Yorkshire, England, were stunned when this curious lenticular cloud appeared in 2011. It was created by the Pennines—the hills forming the country's backbone. Lenticular clouds are a common sight in very mountainous areas, such as the Himalayas, Andes, and Rocky Mountains.

The cloud's base forms where the temperature is cold enough for moisture in the air to condense and form cloud. Below this level, the air is warm, so its moisture stays as invisible vapor.

📊 FAST FACTS

Pressure waves form as air flows over mountains and is forced upward. This creates waves in the same way as a pebble creates ripples in a pond. Lenticular clouds form at the top of the waves, where the air is cool.

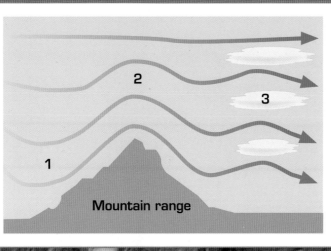

Mountain range

1 Air is forced up and over the mountain range.

2 Air from below disturbs air above and creates waves.

3 Clouds form at the crest of each wave.

Bubbling under

On the surface, **Lake Abraham** in the **Canadian Rocky Mountains** is a photographer's dream. But beneath the frozen waters lie **towers of bubbles**, suspended in ice. These beautiful bubbles hide an ugly secret—they contain **harmful methane gas.**

Lake Abraham's methane bubbles are produced by bacteria on the lake bed feeding on dead plant matter. In the summer, the gas rises to the surface and escapes, but when the lake freezes over, the bubbles are trapped in the ice.

Methane is a greenhouse gas, which traps heat in the atmosphere and contributes to global warming.

Methane gas forms in thousands of lakes. Lake Abraham has high levels because it was created by flooding a valley, so there is a lot of plant matter on the lake bed.

Lake Abraham is an artificial lake, created in 1972 by damming the North Saskatchewan River.

bubbles pile up, as if a bubble-making machine has stopped in mid-flow.

FAST FACTS

Earth's atmosphere allows the sun's heat to reach Earth but stops some from escaping. This is known as the greenhouse effect, and it warms Earth enough to support life. Increasing levels of methane and other greenhouse gases are contributing to the "enhanced greenhouse effect" by trapping more heat and causing Earth's temperature to rise.

Heat from the sun passes through the atmosphere and warms Earth.

Some of the heat escapes into space.

Greenhouse gases trap some of the heat in the atmosphere.

EXPLODING BUBBLES

Methane is a colorless, odorless gas, but it is highly flammable. Scientists studying the frozen bubbles (above) may be unsure which gas they've found. Piercing the ice with a pick and igniting the gas produces explosive results—and proves the gas is methane.

Light show

When Earth's **magnetic field** is disturbed by the sun's solar wind, the night sky lights up with **dancing streaks of color**. While the Northern lights (Aurora borealis) usually steal the show, **the Southern lights** (Aurora australis) are equally impressive but less accessible.

PLANETARY AURORAS

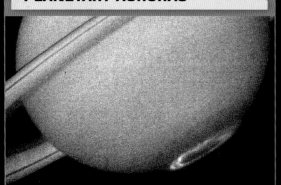

Intrepid explorers can spot auroras in space. Giant Jupiter has a strong magnetic field that reacts with its moons, producing vibrant lights. Saturn has an aurora on its south pole (above), while similar sights have been seen on Uranus, Neptune, and Mars.

This dazzling display of Aurora australis over Antarctica is seen from space.......

Antarctica is surrounded by open water, so there is limited opportunity for people to find a viewing platform from which to enjoy the Aurora australis. ....

Auroras occur when the solar wind—electrically charged particles escaping the sun—becomes trapped by Earth's magnetic field. The particles are funneled toward Earth's two poles, colliding with gases in the atmosphere. These collisions produce Aurora borealis at the north magnetic pole, around the Arctic Circle, and Aurora australis at the south magnetic pole, around the Antarctic Circle.

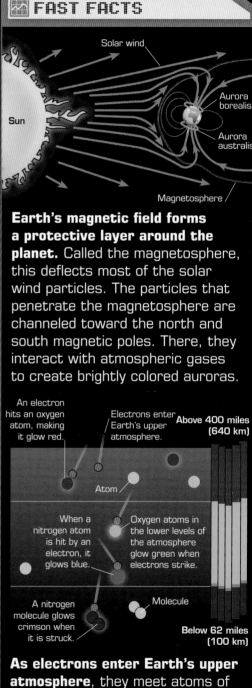

FAST FACTS

Earth's magnetic field forms a protective layer around the planet. Called the magnetosphere, this deflects most of the solar wind particles. The particles that penetrate the magnetosphere are channeled toward the north and south magnetic poles. There, they interact with atmospheric gases to create brightly colored auroras.

An electron hits an oxygen atom, making it glow red.

Electrons enter Earth's upper atmosphere.

Above 400 miles (640 km)

Atom

When a nitrogen atom is hit by an electron, it glows blue.

Oxygen atoms in the lower levels of the atmosphere glow green when electrons strike.

A nitrogen molecule glows crimson when it is struck.

Molecule

Below 62 miles (100 km)

As electrons enter Earth's upper atmosphere, they meet atoms of oxygen and nitrogen at altitudes high above Earth's surface. The color of the aurora depends on which atom is struck, and the altitude of the meeting.

In the past, auroras were considered a premonition of war or plague.

Spiky snow

Resembling an **overgrown garden**, with tall blades of green grass replaced by white snow, penitentes are the **coolest, sharpest snow formations** around. It was once wrongly believed that this **pointy Andes snowscape** was carved out by the biting mountain wind.

Spikes are most plentiful in the areas between Argentina and Chile.

SPIKES IN SPACE

Jupiter's icy moon Europa is thought to be home to penitentes just like those on Earth. These ice blades stretch up to 33 ft (10 m) tall, posing a logistical nightmare for any future spacecraft attempting to land here.

Let's get right to the point—wind doesn't create penitentes. These spikes of hardened snow develop where air is cold and dry, allowing the sun to turn snow instantly into water vapor, without melting it first. This is called sublimation. Some areas sublimate quicker, leaving behind towering penitentes.

The height of penitentes ranges from 1 in (3 cm) up to 16 ft (5 m).

FAST FACTS

The sides of the depressions reflect heat, causing more snow to sublimate.

Tall spikes are created.

Snow sublimates unevenly, creating depressions.

Sunlight turns snow into vapor, creating depressions, which catch more sunlight and so sublimate quicker. The high sides of the depressions become spikes.

English naturalist **Charles Darwin** wrote about **penitentes in 1839**.

Icebreakers

From **giant icebergs** to delicate **frost formations**, ice takes on some strange structures in the world's **coolest places**.

Frost beard
Frost beard resembles silky white hair growing on wood, like this log in Switzerland. Logs absorb rain, but when the water freezes in cold weather, it expands out onto the wooden exterior, exposing icy "hairs."

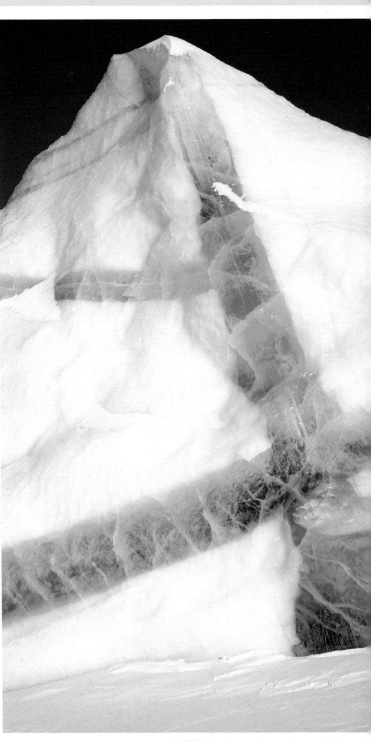

Ice stripes
Icebergs are usually white, but this one in Greenland seems to have blue veins! It is an example of striped ice, which occurs when algae, minerals, or sediment in seawater freeze onto the underside of an iceberg, creating streaks of blue, yellow, brown, or black.

Frost flowers
This pretty but fleeting phenomenon, seen here in the Canadian Rockies, occurs when plants carry water up from their roots to meet surrounding frozen air. Ice crystals form, which spread out and split the plant's stem open to reveal the frozen "flowers."

Polar pancakes
Less tasty than normal pancakes but much bigger, ice pancakes develop in polar regions when bits of foam floating on rivers and oceans freeze and knock into one another. Circular ice blocks result, enjoyed by these ducks on a river in sub-zero Belarus.

Alpine alley

The Tateyama Kurobe Alpine Route is Japan's most spectacular scenic journey. People traveling along **the picturesque passageway** find their view of the lofty mountains suddenly obliterated by towering **snow walls** on either side.

This panoramic route opened in 1971, and is open each year from April to November. It is best known for the staggeringly high snow walls of Murodo, which in some years are as tall as a 10-story building. Other landmark sites along the route include the Kurobe Dam and Hida Mountains.

Diggers clear heavy snow to produce the 65-ft- (20-m-) high Snow Corridor every spring, which stretches for 1,640 ft (500 m).

One million tourists take the Alpine Route each year.

SNOW TUNNELS

In 2015, heavy snowfall in North America resulted in locals digging their own snow tunnels to get out and about. Teams of diggers also constructed a variety of tunnels ranging in depth and length to help commuters and cyclists keep on the move.

FAST FACTS

Mt Tateyama
9,892 ft (3,015 m)

Tateyama Tunnel
Trolleybus

Murodo
Daikanbo
Tateyama
Ropeway
Local
bus

Tengudaira
Kurobe
Dam
Ogizawa

Midagahara
Kurobeko
Omachi
Onsenkyo

Kurobedaira

Kurobe
Cablecar
Kanden Tunnel
Trolleybus

Bijodaira

Tateyama
Highland Bus

Tateyama
Cablecar

Toyama Chiho
Railroad
Tateyama Station

The terrain is tricky on many parts of the 56-mile- (90-km-) long Tateyama Kurobe Alpine Route, so a number of different modes of transportation are used along the way, like trolleybuses, cable cars, and ropeways.

Morning glory

Like a magical highway running straight through the sky, **morning glory clouds** are an **extraordinary weather phenomenon**. A rarity in the rest of the world, they roll around regularly in **remote regions** of northern Australia, caused by wave-like currents in the air.

The spectacular sight can consist of one roll of cloud or as many as 10.

BUBBLING SKIES

When the sky appears to be covered in bubble wrap, it's most likely mammatus clouds. Usually associated with bad weather, these harmless clouds appear as a collection of droopy bulges underneath stormclouds.

These mysterious banks of cloud stretch across the sky from one horizon to the other. Appearing regularly in early morning between September and November, the clouds form in northeastern Australia's Gulf of Carpentaria, and roll in over Burketown, Queensland. The captivating clouds form on waves in the atmosphere created when moist sea air meets a layer of drier air.

The cloud rolls along at speeds of up to 37 mph (60 kph).

Morning glory clouds are a dream come true for hang gliders, who can "surf" them effortlessly, moved by the surrounding thermal winds.

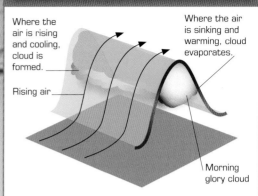

FAST FACTS

Where the air is rising and cooling, cloud is formed.

Where the air is sinking and warming, cloud evaporates.

Rising air

Morning glory cloud

Moisture-laden air blows in from the sea at night, pushing underneath a drier layer of air blown out from the land and creating a wave. Cloud is continuously formed in the upward current of the wave as the moisture-heavy air rises, cools, and condenses. In the downward current, the cloud evaporates. This continuous condensation and evaporation forms the roll-shaped bank of cloud.

Morning glory clouds can be longer than 600 miles (1,000 km).

Snow chimneys

Winter wonderlands can be home to the unexpected sight of **snow chimneys**, or **fumaroles**, puffing steam into the sky. Occurring in **volcanic regions**, fumaroles are openings in Earth's surface from which **hot steam** and volcanic gases are emitted.

Carbon dioxide, sulfur dioxide, and hydrogen sulfide are often emitted from a fumarole, and a gas mask should be worn if confronting these dangerous gases.

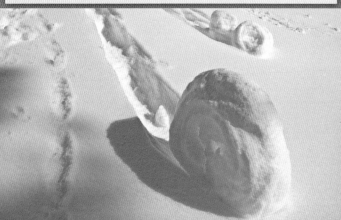

SNOW ROLLERS

Another unusual eye opener is the snow roller. These giant cylinders develop naturally, as smaller pieces of snow blown by high winds gather more snow in a traditional snowballing effect. They are most commonly seen in cold regions of North America and Europe.

Close relations of hot springs and gushing geysers, fumaroles require heat and a gas or water source to burst forth. Volcanic magma (molten rock) under Earth's surface provides the heat and gases. When magma comes into contact with groundwater, the water boils and is released as steam.

Gas can be released for centuries or just a few weeks, depending on the heat source.

FAST FACTS

These steaming vents in Earth's surface always occur in regions with active volcanism. They work in a similar way to geysers: Underground water meets magma and is heated until it boils and bursts through cracks in the rock, making its way to the surface. A fumarole has a smaller reserve of water so emits only steam.

Volcanic eruption

Fumarole

Heated groundwater

Crack

Magma

In Arctic areas, the exiting steam freezes, forming vast snow chimneys around the volcanic opening.

In the line of firenadoes

Beware blazing fires and whirling winds. When two of nature's fiercest foes strike at the same time, they create firenadoes ("fire tornadoes"). Twisting flames leap high into the air in a **dangerous spectacle** that can quickly get out of control.

This firenado started on burning farmland in Chillicothe, Missouri, in 2014.

Shooting flames can stretch 100 ft (30 m) into the sky.

If hot air moves rapidly towards cooler air, it can generate a spiralling vortex (whirlwind). This can happen during a storm, causing a tornado. But a fiercely burning fire can create the same effect, with the added element of flames. These firenadoes do not usually last long, but they can be very destructive, hurling burning ashes over a broad area.

FIREBALL FRENZY

Science struggles to explain the regular occurrence of fireballs exploding from the Mekong River in Thailand. Locals believe that hundreds of "Naga fireballs" are released from the mouth of Naga, a legendary snake said to haunt the waters.

Tornado-like conditions can be created by a raging bush fire. When violent updraughts generated by the fire meet cooler air above, the air starts to spin, forming a funnel.

When the hot updraughts meet cooler air, the air starts to spin.

The intense heat of the bush fire creates violent updraughts.

Oxygen strengthens the flames as the fire is sucked up into the funnel's center, creating a firenado.

Fire and combustible gases are sucked up and fuelled by oxygen in the funnel's center. The funnel turns into a jet of flame—a firenado.

INDEX

ACKNOWLEDGMENTS

Dorling Kindersley would like to thank: Hazel Beynon for proofreading; Jackie Brind for indexing; Carron Brown and Fleur Star for editorial assistance; Rachael Grady, Spencer Holbrook, and Steve Woosnam-Savage for design assistance; Steve Crozier for creative retouching.

The publisher would like to thank the following for their kind permission to reproduce their photographs:

(Key: a–above; b–below/bottom; c–centre; f–far; l–left; r–right; t–top)

1 Ardea: Thomas Marent **2 Corbis:** Paul Williams – Funkystock / imageBROKER (tr). **naturepl.com:** Visuals Unlimited (br). **3 age fotostock:** Iain Masterton (tr). **Alamy Images:** Ivan Kuzmin (c). **Dreamstime.com:** Exposurestonature (bl). **National News and Pictures / National News Press Agency:** Ken Rotberg Photography (cra). **4–5 Corbis:** Paul Williams – Funkystock / imageBROKER. **6 Corbis:** Ulises Rodriguez / epa (br). **6–7 Tormod Sandtorv. 8 Alamy Images:** age fotostock (bl). **8–9 Corbis:** Kazuyoshi Nomachi. **10–11 Getty Images:** Mark D Callanan. **11 Alamy Images:** adp-stock (br). **Dreamstime.com:** Jesús Eloy Ramos Lara (tr). **12 Alamy Images:** All Canada Photos (bl). **12–13 Corbis:** Gunter Marx Photography. **14 Alamy Images:** National Geographic Image Collection (bl). **14–15 National Geographic Creative:** John Stanmeyer. **16–17 123RF.com:** derege. **17 Alamy Images:** Sergey Podkolzin (tc). **18–19 Corbis:** Imaginechina. **18 Corbis:** Viking 1 (bl). **20 Corbis:** Michele Falzone / JAI (b). **21 Fotolia:** janmiko (bl). **Getty Images:** Suzanne and Nick Geary (cr). **Masterfile:** Frank Krahmer (tr). **22–23 Alamy Images:** blickwinkel. **22 NASA:** JPL / Space Science Institute (bl). **24–25 Alfred-Wegener-Institute for Polar and Marine Research. 25 Corbis:** George Steinmetz (br). **26–27 Corbis:** Christophe Boisvieux / Hemis. **27 Corbis:** Christophe Boisvieux (br). **28–29 Corbis:** Martin Harvey. **29 FLPA:** Chien Lee / Minden Pictures (br). **30 Corbis:** Marco Stoppato & Amanda Ronzoni / Visuals Unlimited (bl). **32–33 7ty9 / flickr. 33 Getty Images:** Barcroft Media (br). **34–35 Iurie Belegurschi. 35 Corbis:** Aaron McCoy / Robert Harding World Imagery (br). **36–37 Caters News Agency:** Mikhail Mishainik (b). **37 Getty Images:** Linde Waidehofer / Barcroft Media (cr). **Science Photo Library:** Javier Trueba / MSF (tr). **38 National Geographic Creative:** Stephen Alvarez (bl). **38–39 National**

Geographic Creative: Stephen Alvarez. **40–41 FLPA:** Gerry Ellis / Minden Pictures. **41 Corbis:** Anup Shah (bl). **42–43 AWL Images:** Paul Harris. **42 Corbis:** Jason Reeve / Demotix (bl). **44–45 age fotostock:** Iain Masterton. **46–47 AWL Images:** Max Milligan. **47 DK Images:** Angela Coppola / University of Pennsylvania Museum of Archaeology and Anthropology (bc). **48–49 Alamy Images:** Paul Springett 10. **48 Rex Features:** Imaginechina (bl). **50 Alamy Images:** dpa picture alliance archive (b). **Corbis:** Wolfgang Rattay / Reuters (cl). **51 Corbis:** Wolfgang Rattay / Reuters (br). **Getty Images:** William West / AFP (tl). **TopFoto.co.uk:** ullsteinbild (cl). **52–53 Stuart Jackson Carter. 53 Corbis:** Marc Dozier (bc). **54 Alamy Images:** Blaine Harrington III (cr). **54–55 Getty Images:** Moment Open. **56–57 Gavin Thurston. 57 Rex Features:** Paul Raffaele (bl). **58 Getty Images:** Timothy Allen (bl). **58–59 Frederic Buyle:** (tr). **60–61 Getty Images:** Timothy Allen. **60 Rex Features:** HAP / Quirky China News (bl). **62 Alamy Images:** Pacific Press. **62–63 Dima Chatrov. 64–65 Alamy Images:** Prisma Bildagentur AG. **65 Getty Images:** Sergio Camacho (br). **66–67 Getty Images:** Juergen Richter / LOOK-foto. **66 Rex Features:** Liam Kidston / Newspix (cl). **68–69 Corbis:** Chaiwat Subprasom / Reuters (b). **69 age fotostock:** Danita Delimont Agency (cr). **Getty Images:** Eye Ubiquitous / Contributor (tl).

70 Alamy Images: Hemis (bl). **70–71 Corbis:** Steve Kaufman. **72 Getty Images:** Patrick Aventurier / Gamma-Rapho (bl). **72–73 Alamy Images:** Jim Kidd. **74–75 Alamy Images:** Steve Davey Photography. **75 Alamy Images:** Danita Delimont (cr). **76–77 Google. 76 Google:** Street View (bl). **78–79 Getty Images:** Stringer / AFP. **79 Alamy Images:** Robert Harding World Imagery (bl). **80–81 Corbis:** epa. **81 Corbis:** Michael Buholzer / Reuters (tr). **82–83 Alamy Images:** David R. Frazier Photolibrary, Inc.. **82 Alamy Images:** Nancy Hoyt Belcher (bl). **84–85 Corbis:** LWA / Larry Williams / Blend Images. **85 Alamy Images:** Jon Arnold Images Ltd (tl). **86–87 Dreamstime.com:** Exposurestonature. **88–89 Corbis:** Alcibbum Photography. **89 Andrea Moro:** (tr). **90–91 Science Photo Library:** Dr Morley Read. **90 laajala/flickr:** (bl). **92 Caters News Agency:** Eeerkia Schulz (b). **93 Alamy Images:** age fotostock (bl); David Bigwood (cr). **NOLEHACE Orchid Photography:** (tr). **94 FLPA:** Photo Researchers (l). **94–95 FLPA:** Photo Researchers (b). **95 Corbis:** Ch'ien Lee / Minden Pictures (br).

FLPA: Photo Researchers (r). **96–97 Rex Features:** Amos Chapple. **96 Pooktre / Peter Cook and Becky Northey:** (tl). **98–99 SuperStock:** Sara Janini / age fotostock. **98 SuperStock:** Morales / age fotostock (bl). **100–101 Getty Images:** Cultura Travel / Romona Robbins Photography (b). **101 Alamy Images:** Prisma Bildagentur AG (l); Susan Pease (cr). **102 Alamy Images:** Ecoimage (bl). **102–103 GAP Photos:** Richard Wareham. **104–105 Alamy Images:** epa european pressphoto agency b.v.. **105 Getty Images:** Lam Yik Fei (bc). **106–107 Corbis:** Taylor Lockwood / Visuals Unlimited. **107 biology-forums.com:** (bl). **108 Alamy Images:** imageBROKER (bl). **Corbis:** Josef Beck / imageBROKER (cr). **109 Alamy Images:** Arco Images GmbH (cl). **Corbis:** Ch'ien Lee / Minden Pictures (r). **110 Corbis:** Marc Dozier (cl). **110–111 Getty Images:** Blend Images. **112–113 Corbis:** Doug Perrine / Nature Picture Library. **113 Science Photo Library:** Brian Brake (crb). **114–115 Alamy Images:** Ivan Kuzmin. **116 Corbis:** Michael Durham / Minden Pictures (bl). **116–117 Caters News Agency:** Gary Tindale. **118–119 Caters News Agency:** Antero Topp. **119 Photoshot:** NHPA (br). **120 Alamy Images:** Ethan Daniels (b). **121 Corbis:** Juan Medina / Reuters (tl); Michael Edwards / Great Stock (br). **Rex Features:** Mint Images (cl). **122–123 FLPA:** Frans Lanting. **123 Alamy Images:** Marvin Dembinsky Photo Associates (cr). **124–125 Corbis:** Department for International Development / Russell Watkins. **125 Corbis:** Stephen Frink (br). **Jurgen Otto. 127 Corbis:** Tim Laman / National Geographic Creative (br). **128 Corbis:** Dr. David Phillips / Visuals Unlimited (br). **128–129 Science Photo Library:** Eye Of Science. **129 Science Photo Library:** Eye Of Science (br). **130 Alamy Images:** Ethan Daniels (b). **131 Alamy Images:** Frank Hecker (cl); Michael Doolittle (tr). **FLPA:** Gianpiero Ferrari (br). **132–133 Science Photo Library:** Eye Of Science. **133 Alamy Images:** Science Photo Library (br). **134–135 Science Photo Library:** Dr George Beccaloni. **135 Richard Seaman:** (tr). **136 Corbis:** Michael Weber / imageBROKER (bl). **136–137 naturepl.com:** Visuals Unlimited. **137 Getty Images:** Visuals Unlimited, Inc. / Thomas Marent. **138–139 Ardea:** Thomas Marent. **139 Alamy Images:** Scott Buckel (tr). **140–141 FLPA:** Matthias Breiter / Minden Pictures (b); Thomas Marent / Minden Pictures (t). **140 Getty Images:** Gallo Images (cl). **141 Dreamstime.com:** Seatraveler (tr). **FLPA:** Gianpiero Ferrari (br).

142–143 Alamy Images: Paul Strawson. **143 Alamy Images:** AGF Srl (bl). **144 FLPA:** Hugh Lansdown. **Getty Images:** Jim Abernethy (bl). **145 FLPA:** Hugh Lansdown (l, r). **146 Press Association Images:** Peter Morrison / AP (bl). **146–147 Martin Le-May. 148 FLPA:** Kelvin Aitken / Biosphoto (bl). **148–149 OceanwideImages.com:** Rudie Kuiter. **150–151 Science Photo Library:** Christopher Swann. **151 Alamy Images:** WaterFrame (bl). **152 Corbis:** Larry Madin / WHOI / Visuals Unlimited (b). **153 Corbis:** Wim van Egmond / Visuals Unlimited (tl). **FLPA:** Norbert Wu / Minden Pictures (br). **Science Photo Library:** Dante Fenolio (cl). **154–155 National News and Pictures / National News Press Agency:** Ken Rotberg Photography. **156–157 Alamy Images:** Mark Tomalty / Aurora Photos. **156 SuperStock:** Prisma (bl). **158 Dreamstime.com:** Sean Pavone (cr). **158–159 Alamy Images:** Carver Mostardi. **160–161 Press Association Images:** Jad Saab / AP. **161 Alamy Images:** John Warburton-Lee Photography (tr). **162–163 Alamy Images:** imageBROKER. **162 Corbis:** Tourism Ministry / Xinhua Press (tl). **164–165 Stephen Locke. 165 Alamy Images:** Thierry Grun (cr). **166 Corbis:** Mike Theiss / Ultimate Chase (cl). **166–167 Corbis:** Reuters (tr); Wave (b). **167 Corbis:** Eric Nguyen (tr). **Press Association Images:** Stephen B. Thornton / AP (br). **168–169 Martin Rietze. 168 NASA:** JPL / University of Arizona (bl). **170 Dreamstime.com:** Matt Dobson (bl). **170–171 Brian Middleton. 172–173 Getty Images:** Photographer's Choice. **173 Corbis:** Mark Thiessen / National Geographic Creative (br). **174–175 Science Photo Library:** NASA. **174 NASA:** ESA / J.T. Trauger (Jet Propulsion Laboratory) (bl). **176 NASA:** JPL-Caltech / SETI Institute (bl). **176–177 Stephan Kenzelmann. 178 Alamy Images:** blickwinkel (br). **Getty Images:** Thomas Marent (cl). **179 Corbis:** Tatyana Zenkovich / epa (br). **Getty Images:** Photolibrary (t). **180–181 Getty Images:** UniversalImagesGroup / Contributor (cl). **181 Corbis:** CJ Gunther / epa (tr). **182–183 Mick Petroff. 184–185 Corbis:** Gerald & Buff Corsi / Visuals Unlimited. **184 National Geographic Creative:** George Steinmetz (bl). **186 Alamy Images:** Triangle Travels (br). **186–187 Barcroft Media Ltd.:** Janae Copelin

All other images © Dorling Kindersley

For further information see: **www.dkimages.com**